*A LifeBuilder*

EVANGELISM
A Way of Life

12 studies
for individuals or groups

Rebecca Manley Pippert
& Ruth Siemens

With Notes for Leaders

Scripture Union is an international Christian charity working with churches in more than 130 countries.

Thank you for purchasing this book. Any profits from this book support SU in England and Wales to bring the good news of Jesus Christ to children, young people and families and to enable them to meet God through the Bible and prayer.

Find out more about our work and how you can get involved at:

www.scriptureunion.org.uk (England and Wales)
www.suscotland.org.uk (Scotland)
www.suni.org (Northern Ireland)
www.scriptureunion.org (USA)
www.su.org.au (Australia)

ISBN 978 1 85999 484 9

First published in the United States by InterVarsity Press.
Published in Great Britain by Scripture Union 2001, reprinted 2004, 2006, 2011, 2012.

© all editions Rebecca Manley Pippert & Ruth Siemens

British Library Cataloguing-in-Publication data: a catalogue record for this book is available from the British Library.

Printed in India by Thomson Press India Ltd.

Contents

Getting the Most Out of *Evangelism*

One day on a plane I happened to sit next to a rather intellectual-looking professor. We leaped into a stimulating conversation, and I intended to tell him about my faith—at the appropriate time. But abruptly he asked me what I did for a living. I said, "Well, I'm in Christian work." (It's one thing to be a Christian; another thing to do it for a living.)

A look of amazement spread across his face. He was clearly thinking, *Funny—she* looked *so normal!* Immediately his demeanor changed, and he was clearly trying to find the appropriate words to use for a "Christian type." He asked, with the slightest condescension, "Well, what's the name of your little organization?"

"InterVarsity Christian Fellowship," I replied. He looked bewildered. I asked, "Is something wrong?"

He said, "Oh, nothing really. It's just . . . well . . . you don't *look* like a Christian athlete."

Thinking at that point that he was joking, I said, "Well, yes, I play basketball for Jesus. It's a living."

Without a hesitation he said, "Oh, I'm sure it must be very rewarding."

It was a great temptation to play along with his feigned religious behavior and say, "Yes, well, it's such a little blessing. You know, we never lose a game." However, with uncommon restraint, I told him, "No, actually that was a joke. We make jokes sometimes. However, you asked me if my work is rewarding. I would prefer to say it is terribly intriguing."

And almost in spite of himself he asked, "Intriguing? Well, *why* is that?"

I answered, "Because I work with students. And we constantly face the question 'How do we know anything is true? How do we know that we aren't taking our own little world and labeling it reality? Is there any basis for our faith or is it mere wish fulfillment?'"

He answered, "You may not believe this, but those questions were going through my mind as well. Okay. What kind of evidences *do* you have?" And so we talked about the evidence for Christian faith. Then he said, "You know, besides the evidence I think what impresses me most in this conversation is that you seem to be a person of hope and not despair. Why is that?"

Then I was able to share for the last five minutes of our descent that the reason is Jesus Christ.

My experience with the professor was vastly different from my embarrassment in first sharing the gospel. At that time I was in Spain as an undergraduate student. I knew God had called me to be a witness, but for the first several months I allowed the fears and insecurities of sharing Christ, as well as my discomfort with being a witness in a different culture and a different language, to intimidate me.

For example, one day I was reading the Bible for my devotions when a cynical friend entered my room unexpectedly and said, "¿Que estas leyendo?" (What are you reading?)

I was sure she would think I was a religious fanatic—not only reading my Bible but on a weekday! So I quickly slipped my Bible under other books and tried to look as cool as possible. "Oh, nothing, really."

"Yes you were. What were you reading?"

"Oh, not much," I answered.

"Becky, what were you *reading*?" she demanded.

"All right! It's the Bible!" I confessed. (And I behaved this way so she would not think I was strange!)

I slowly began to realize that we are called to expose our faith, not impose it or hide it. As I read the Gospels and saw how beautifully Jesus dealt with people, it began to free me up.

It's a long story, but God gave me an antidote for my fears and timidity about sharing my faith. By the time I left Spain, God used a Bible study that I was leading to win five people (including avowed atheists and one

Marxist) to Christ. Until that time I had never seen one person become a Christian. Today I am the godmother of one of the former atheists' children. If you had asked me at the time if any of those five students seemed open to God, I would have laughed out loud. But I could not see their hearts, nor the power of God's Spirit to penetrate their hearts.

Since that experience in Spain I have seen many people turn their lives over to God and be changed. And yet the awesome miracle of conversion never fails to move me. What can be more miraculous than seeing a person who was once dead in sin become alive to God?

Even more remarkable is that God invites us to be a part of that process. We not only have the honor of sharing God's message, but we even have the awesome privilege of inviting a response. It is because of the enormity of this privilege that Ruth Siemens and I have written these Bible studies.

How do we get to the point of discussing Jesus Christ with our friends or with strangers? And how can we overcome our fears and insecurities about evangelism? How do we find the boldness and confident faith that we need? This study guide helps us answer these questions. It consists of twelve studies which look at the example of Jesus and the early evangelists. They teach us how to communicate the gospel clearly and creatively.

I have written these studies with Ruth Siemens, my former housemate in Spain. Ruth helped me get over my initial fears about sharing my faith in Jesus Christ. With great wisdom, encouragement and patience she helped me see that evangelism can be a way of life.

Suggestions for Individual Study

1. As you begin each study, pray that God will speak to you through his Word.

2. Read the introduction to the study and respond to the personal reflection question or exercise. This is designed to help you focus on God and on the theme of the study.

3. Each study deals with a particular passage—so that you can delve into the author's meaning in that context. Read and reread the passage to be studied. If you are studying a book, it will be helpful to read through the entire book prior to the first study. The questions are written using the language of the New International Version, so you may wish to use that version of the Bible. The New Revised Standard Version is also recommended.

4. This is an inductive Bible study, designed to help you discover for yourself what Scripture is saying. The study includes three types of questions. *Observation* questions ask about the basic facts: who, what, when, where and how. *Interpretation* questions delve into the meaning of the passage. *Application* questions help you discover the implications of the text for growing in Christ. These three keys unlock the treasures of Scripture.

Write your answers to the questions in the spaces provided or in a personal journal. Writing can bring clarity and deeper understanding of yourself and of God's Word.

5. It might be good to have a Bible dictionary handy. Use it to look up any unfamiliar words, names or places.

6. Use the prayer suggestion to guide you in thanking God for what you have learned and to pray about the applications that have come to mind.

7. You may want to go on to the suggestion under "Now or Later," or you may want to use that idea for your next study.

Suggestions for Members of a Group Study

1. Come to the study prepared. Follow the suggestions for individual study mentioned above. You will find that careful preparation will greatly enrich your time spent in group discussion.

2. Be willing to participate in the discussion. The leader of your group will not be lecturing. Instead, he or she will be encouraging the members of the group to discuss what they have learned. The leader will be asking the questions that are found in this guide.

3. Stick to the topic being discussed. Your answers should be based on the verses which are the focus of the discussion and not on outside authorities such as commentaries or speakers. These studies focus on a particular passage of Scripture. Only rarely should you refer to other portions of the Bible. This allows for everyone to participate in in-depth study on equal ground.

4. Be sensitive to the other members of the group. Listen attentively when they describe what they have learned. You may be surprised by their insights! Each question assumes a variety of answers. Many questions do not have "right" answers, particularly questions that aim at meaning or application. Instead the questions push us to explore the passage more thoroughly.

When possible, link what you say to the comments of others. Also, be affirming whenever you can. This will encourage some of the more hesitant members of the group to participate.

5. Be careful not to dominate the discussion. We are sometimes so eager to express our thoughts that we leave too little opportunity for others to respond. By all means participate! But allow others to also.

6. Expect God to teach you through the passage being discussed and through the other members of the group. Pray that you will have an enjoyable and profitable time together, but also that as a result of the study you will find ways that you can take action individually and/or as a group.

7. Remember that anything said in the group is considered confidential and should not be discussed outside the group unless specific permission is given to do so.

8. If you are the group leader, you will find additional suggestions at the back of the guide.

1

Why Spread the Good News?

I once saw the great Russian ballet dancer Mikael Baryshnikov dance to Ballanchine's choreographed rendition of "The Prodigal Son." The most powerful moment of the ballet came when Baryshnikov, playing the prodigal and dressed in a skeletonlike leotard, returns to beg forgiveness from his father. In the closing moments of the ballet as the father cradles his son tenderly in his arms, we watch the son rest his head on his father's chest in exhausted comfort. He is home at last, and that is all that matters.

Why does this story of Jesus, told to orthodox Jewish believers over two thousand years ago, still pack such a wallop, even today? Because Jesus taps into the deepest, most primal of human emotions: *there's a child in desperate trouble*. And as a result, relationships in the family have been broken, parents are grieving, anxiety abounds. Will the lost child find his way home again? Will the parents' broken hearts be mended? Will the child be restored and become whole?

GROUP DISCUSSION. Think of a time you lost something extremely valuable and precious. How did you feel? Was it returned? If so, describe your feelings.

PERSONAL REFLECTION. How do you regard unbelievers who have

messy lives—with compassion or with a judgmental, critical spirit? Why?

The parable we are going to read is set in a context of three stories. First, Jesus tells us that a shepherd has lost one of his one hundred sheep. He goes to great lengths to find that lost sheep and when he finds it he rejoices greatly. Jesus then says, "There will be more joy in heaven over one sinner who repents than over ninety-nine righteous persons who do not need to repent" (Luke 15:7). In other words, God's desire to find sinners and bring them back into the fold is beyond what we could fathom.

Next, Jesus tells the story of the woman who lost a coin. She searches thoroughly with the aid of a lamp until it turns up. The implication is that disciples should diligently engage in the search for sinners on behalf of the Great Shepherd they serve.

In the parable of the prodigal son we continue to see the seeking-of-sinners theme that helps us understand our proper motive for sharing the good news. *Read Luke 15:1-2, 11-32.*

---

1. Why did Jesus feel the need to tell this story?

---

2. The inheritance was normally given to sons after the death of the father. The younger son's share would be one-third and the older son's two-thirds of the father's wealth (Deuteronomy 21:17). How do you think the Jewish crowd who was listening to the story felt in hearing that the younger son pushed for his share of the inheritance (vv. 11-12)?

---

3. In the Jewish culture of Jesus' day, children were not only raised to obey the law but to stay close as a family unit. How would the Pharisees react on hearing the further antics of this son (v. 13)?

4. How would the boy's job be the worst imaginable occupation for a child who was probably raised in a kosher kitchen (vv. 14-15)?

5. This boy's actions would have been utterly repelling to the listeners. What types of people do you find hard to reach out to?

6. What do you think led this boy into sin and rebellion?

7. How does Jesus describe the nature of repentance?

Although repentance is always a mystery in the end, what factors seemed to influence the son's repentance?

8. After hearing a story in which Jesus deliberately pressed all their buttons, what might the Pharisees and teachers of the law expect the father's response to be?

9. Jesus gives us one of the most beautiful portraits of God the Father seen in Scripture. Name everything that the father does (vv. 20-24).

10. Jesus' point is that we are so precious to God and he is so loving by nature that the mere act of repentance brings an absolute reversal of status. The lost son has become a family member again. The father's acceptance of the penitent son is total. How does this radical view of God's grace square with your understanding of God's attitude toward you?

---

11. What was wrong with the elder son's understanding and experience of faith that he refused to go the party (vv. 25-30)?

---

12. Why is a judgmental, critical spirit so frequently the "disease of the devoted," as was the case of the Pharisees?

---

13. Reflect on the father's response of complete joy to his son's return. How can you allow this attitude to shape your attitude toward people you find repelling?

Thank the Lord for the many ways he has delivered you from evil and shown you mercy in spite of your sins. Ask him to enlarge your heart so that his compassion and love will flow through you to those who have not found their way home yet.

Now or Later
Take time to thank God with your whole heart for your salvation. Try to imagine yourself as a "mouse in the corner" in heaven when God threw a celebration party for your conversion. Thank God for each person he used to reach you.

2

A Life
That Speaks

Colossians 3:5—4:6

Most of us are uncomfortable invading the privacy of people and imposing on them a religious conversation they may not want. In contrast the apostle Paul teaches us an effective nonintrusive approach that gets seekers to ask questions. He focuses on our godly character, conduct and conversation. We should not underestimate the power of a Christ-filled life. It turns out that our lives are our most powerful evangelism tool.

GROUP DISCUSSION. What are some reasons that Christians don't talk about Jesus Christ?

PERSONAL REFLECTION. What area of weakness in evangelism do you struggle with?

Paul wrote this letter from Rome, where he had just been moved to Nero's palace prison to await trial for preaching the gospel. (There he evangelized the whole praetorian guard and won converts in Caesar's household.) He writes to new churches founded by his convert Epaphras in Colosse, Laodicea and Hierapolis (in modern Turkey). Since Paul's emphasis is on lifestyle, not techniques, his ethical teachings in all of his letters become evangelism training—checklists for witness in each of our circles: work, campus, neighborhood and clubs. *Read Colossians 3:5—4:1.*

1. Looking through the passage, what are some bad habits (implicit and explicit) that these expagan believers must now eliminate?

2. How would seeing these lifestyle changes in the believers affect pagan outsiders?

3. Paul had told them in 1:27 that the great "mystery," the secret of the Christian life, was "Christ in you, the hope of glory!" What beautiful qualities was Christ producing in the believers he now indwelt by his Spirit (vv. 12-17)?

4. When have you seen the power of someone's witness following a dramatic change in lifestyle?

5. Notice what Paul says in 3:11 about discrimination. What new facts made such a radical reorientation of all Christian relationships both possible and necessary?

6. Why would outsiders find the Christians' collective witness (their behavior together and toward each other) even more thirst-producing and question-inducing than their individual conduct?

7. In verses 15 and 17, Paul makes an issue of thanking God in everything. How does this transform even our most menial, boring or challenging tasks?

8. The main social unit was the "household"—a man's family, house servants, farm laborers, artisans who ran businesses, even a tutor, doctor and lawyer. They were all the man's property. What surprising instructions does Paul give householders?

How would their transformation affect their owner?

9. What new standard was to govern the attitudes of slaves? How does this apply to us in our work place?

10. *Read Colossians 4:2-6.* According to Paul, how will the Christians' truly "wise" conduct and gracious conversations affect the outsiders (nonbelievers) around them?

11. Instead of imposing religious conversations on people who might be offended, what are several advantages if we can get them to ask us questions about our faith?

12. Seeing the winsome, godly conduct of Christians can turn indifferent and hostile people into seekers as effectively today as in the first century. If nonbelievers in your social circles are not asking questions about your faith, what are possible reasons?

What steps toward change would you like to take?

Ask the Lord to help you live out the gospel and make fitting comments in each of your social circles so that you might win seekers to the Lord.

Now or Later

Take an hour or so to read through the following passages and pick out everything that can help improve your conduct and relationships with seekers: Colossians 3:1-4; Ephesians 4:17—6:19; 2 Corinthians 3:1-3; Galatians 6:9-10; Philippians 4:4-9; 1 Timothy 3:5-6; Titus 1-3; Romans 12:9—13:14.

3

Getting People Interested

John 4:4-30

"Evangelism is not the imposition of a point of view but the overflow of a thankful heart."*

Christians sometimes communicate their faith as if they are sales people trying to sell a product. But evangelism is not employing a super sales strategy. Why? Because the gospel is not for sale! It is a free gift of grace for those who will accept it. We are called to *expose* our faith in the most winsome way possible—not impose it.

GROUP DISCUSSION. What kinds of people make you feel they'd never be interested in the gospel?

PERSONAL REFLECTION. What are specific skills you need to develop to become a better communicator of the gospel?

Have you ever met a person and instantly concluded, "Oh, they'd never be interested in the gospel," only to discover later how wrong you were? If you have, then you're in good company. The disciples crossed the Samaritan woman off their list because a mere glance betrayed her immoral life and her Samaritan racial characteristics. But Jesus shows us that we must never look at a person superficially. Instead, we should ask ourselves, *Why are they doing what they do?*

Are they looking for the right thing but in all the wrong places? If that is the case, then the real challenge before us is how to arouse their curiosity in the gospel. *Read John 4:4-30.*

1. While Jesus is resting from his journey, a Samaritan woman approaches at "the sixth hour" (noon). Why would she come to draw water at the hottest time of the day (vv. 6-7)?

2. The Jews had high standards of righteousness that they thought their rabbis should live up to. How does Jesus arouse the woman's curiosity by taking the risk of talking to her?

3. Instead of telling her right away who he was, Jesus began by asking the woman for a favor (v. 7). How has an unbeliever surprised you by meeting your needs?

4. Why does Jesus' use the phrase "living water" when he knows she won't fully comprehend his meaning (vv. 11-15)?

5. Why, just at this strategic moment when the women says she'll take this water he is offering, does Jesus delve into her personal life (vv. 16-18)?

6. What relationships do you now see between the "thirst" Jesus has been speaking of and the woman's immoral past?

7. Think of seekers you know. In what ways do they indicate they are spiritually thirsty?

How can you show them the way the gospel can meet their needs without being judgmental or manipulative? (Note that even though Jesus speaks frankly about the woman's morals, she does not respond defensively.)

8. The Samaritans worshiped on Mount Gerizim, the Jews in Jerusalem. How does Jesus deal with the woman's "red herring" in verses 19-24?

9. Why does Jesus wait until the end of the conversation to reveal who he is (vv. 25-26)?

10. How do verses 28-30 reveal the woman's excitement about her conversation with Jesus?

11. Look back over the passage. What are the ways Jesus aroused the woman's interest in the good news?

12. How can we use objects, ideas, experiences and needs people are familiar with to arouse interest in spiritual truths? Give some specific examples of how you might arouse someone's interest in the gospel.

Ask God to open your eyes and help you see "beneath the crust" of the lives of the seekers you know. Pray that he will help you recognize their God-hunger and make you more effective in being a "fisher" not a "hunter" of people.

Now or Later

Ask the Lord to show you who the spiritually receptive people are in your life right now. Invite one person to do something socially with you this week. Then, if you feel led, throw out a comment or two about spiritual things, see how they respond and go from there.

*Donald G. Bloesch, *A Theology of Word & Spirit* (Downers Grove, Ill.: InterVarsity Press, 1992), p. 244.

4

The Good News

The heart of evangelism is sharing the story of Christ, the good news of how God took upon himself the sin and shame of the human race so that all who believe in him might be saved. This message is the most liberating news to ever grace this planet. Dietrich Bonhoeffer wrote, "To tell others that the cause is urgent, and that the kingdom of God is at hand is the most charitable and merciful act we can perform, the most joyous news we can bring."*

The early evangelists felt that way about the gospel. They wanted to tell everyone the good news of what God has done for us through Jesus Christ. If we are to recapture their sense of wonder and excitement, we too must grasp what Jesus has done and realize that it is the best news people will ever hear.

GROUP DISCUSSION. Apart from the gospel, what is some of the best news you have ever received? How did it make you feel?

PERSONAL REFLECTION. If a seeker asked you to explain the gospel briefly and concisely, would you be able to do it? What aspects of the message would you need help in understanding?

This passage is of particular interest in our postmodern age, for this story is about as politically incorrect as one can get! Here's a story about a genuinely nice guy, a religious man who prays and gives to the poor, who is of another race and, we assume, was raised in a different religious tradition before he became a God-fearer. So shouldn't Peter simply accept him as he is? In this story we see as never before that the gospel of Jesus Christ is for all people—Jews as well as Gentiles. And Peter was as surprised to learn this as Cornelius! *Read Acts 10:1-2, 23-48.*

1. From these verses, how would you describe Cornelius?

2. What evidence is there that Cornelius was eagerly awaiting Peter's arrival (vv. 23-26)?

3. What circumstances brought this scrupulous Jew into the home of a Gentile (vv. 27-33)?

4. These circumstances helped to overturn Peter's sense of racial superiority (vv. 34-35). Why is it important to realize that the gospel transcends racial, economic, social and political barriers?

5. Peter begins his message to these Gentiles by characterizing the gospel as "the good news of peace through Jesus Christ, who is Lord of all" (v. 36). He then summarizes Jesus' three-year ministry in verses 37-38. How do these verses capture the essence of Jesus' ministry?

6. Deuteronomy 21:23 states that "anyone who is hung on a tree is under God's curse." How would you explain to someone today why Jesus, who was anointed and blessed by God, died under his curse (v. 39)?

7. How would you explain to a friend why it is significant that God raised Jesus from the dead (v. 40)?

8. Twice Peter mentions that he and others are "witnesses" of what he is describing (vv. 39, 41). Why do you think he stresses this fact?

9. God commanded the apostles to testify that Jesus will judge the living and the dead (v. 42). How does this "bad news" highlight the good news in verse 43?

10. How would you explain to someone what it means to *believe* in Jesus (v. 43)?

11. Verses 44-46 have been called the "Pentecost of the Gentile world." Why was this event significant for both Peter and those who experienced it?

12. In this passage God goes to extraordinary lengths to spread the good news. This emphasizes the importance he places on the message of salvation. What can you do to learn the gospel message better?

Pray that God will give you the courage to be bold in sharing the gospel even if it seems politically incorrect to do so. Ask him to fill you anew with the Spirit's power and anointing as you share the gospel with others.

Now or Later

Can you find these same core truths in other beautiful formulations of the gospel in the Bible? Try Acts 2:22-24, 38,39; Acts 4:30-32; John 3:16-21; Colossians 2:13-15.

---

*Dietrich Bonhoeffer, *The Cost of Discipleship*, trans. R. H. Fuller (London: SCM Press, 1959), p. 165.

5

Creative Communication

G. K. Chesterton once said, "Christianity is not simply difficult—it's impossible." The truth is, because the cancer of sin has infected all of the human race, no one can obey God's commandments apart from God's power. But the challenge is helping seekers understand that, as Romans 3:23 says, "all have sinned and fall short of the glory of God." This is a particularly vital issue since sin tends to build up its own defenses that can be difficult for the truth to penetrate. We need to find strategies that can scale the defenses of sin and slip past its armor. That is why Jesus often employed parables.

GROUP DISCUSSION. Communication theorists tell us that we learn in a variety of ways. For example, some need their intellects aroused, some like to be challenged to action and some need their imagination sparked. What stimulates you to learn?

PERSONAL REFLECTION. What are your central strengths in communication the gospel? What are the areas you would most like to improve?

Have you ever met a skeptic who listens to you talk about Christ in passive silence, and you just can't get him to interact with you? Or do you know someone who enjoys discussing the faith on an intellectual level only, yet you are unable to get her actively involved? Or maybe you've got a friend who is content and satisfied with life, and you can't figure out how to help him see his need for Jesus. Jesus' answers to a lawyer's questions offer some clues on how to deal with each of these situations. *Read Luke 10:25-37.*

1. Notice the questions the expert poses to Jesus throughout this passage. What do you learn about him?

2. Jesus could simply have said that eternal life comes from surrender and faith in him. Instead, he asks the man a question (v. 26). Why?

How can asking good questions help us to communicate the gospel more effectively?

3. What does the lawyer's answer reveal about his understanding of eternal life (v. 27)?

4. When the lawyer answers "correctly," Jesus tells him to act on what he already knows to be true (v. 28). Why do you think the lawyer becomes defensive at this point (v. 29)?

5. In order to feel the impact of Jesus' parable, we must look through the eyes of the lawyer. How would he have expected a priest, a Levite and a Samaritan to respond to the man's needs? Explain why.

6. Why do you think the priest and Levite "passed by on the other side" instead of helping the man?

7. How should our relationship with God affect how we relate to people and keep us from passing by those in need?

8. How does the Samaritan demonstrate the meaning of "love your neighbor as yourself" (vv. 33-35)?

9. Why does Jesus tell a story and then challenge the lawyer to put into practice the truth he believes?

10. Suppose this specialist in Jewish law took Jesus' challenge and set out to love God and his neighbor as never before, but then he discovered his inadequacy in putting this truth into practice. How might a second conversation with Jesus be different?

11. God frequently uses two strategies in the Bible to get people's attention: he asks questions, and tells stories. Yet Christians often give answers and preach sermons. How can you make your communication more in keeping with God's way?

12. What biblical stories or personal illustrations and examples could you use to be more effective in sharing the gospel?

Ask God to help you learn that you don't have to verbally dominate a witnessing opportunity to be effective. Pray that the Spirit would help you to ask the right questions and free you to tell God's story and your story with greater effectiveness.

Now or Later

Read the next story of Mary and Martha. Why does Luke put this story immediately after the story of the lawyer? How does Jesus' response to Martha reveal the truth that the lawyer needs to learn.

6

An Unlikely
Seeker

Luke 19:1-11

Did you ever sing "Zacchaeus was a wee little man" in Sunday school? A simple gospel narrative can delight us when we are children and surprise us with its practical, theological content when we are adults. This story of an unlikely seeker provides valuable insights for evangelism.

GROUP DISCUSSION. If you want to give a seeker the good news, what kind of person do you tend to look for? What kinds of people might you bypass because they intimidate you?

PERSONAL REFLECTION. If a seeker asked you how to become a Christian, how would you respond?

Jesus is on his way to Jerusalem for Passover. Huge crowds accompany him. The celebration begins enroute. This religious festival was obligatory for all men within traveling distance, and many came from abroad. In Jerusalem visitors camped out in tiny makeshift tents on streets and squares and rooftops. The city would swell to several times its size—and this was no ordinary year. People thought the kingdom of God would appear at once (Luke 19:11)! They expected that Jesus, God's King, would free them from Rome, oust the Gentiles and make the Jews rich. *Read Luke 19:1-11.*

1. From verses 1-4 find all the facts you can about Zacchaeus.

2. What has Zacchaeus heard and believed about Jesus to make him so desperate to see him (vv. 3, 4, 11)?

3. Picture what the crowd does when Jesus stops and looks up into the tree. What mixed feelings would Zacchaeus have had as he was caught in the tree and as he heard Jesus' words (vv. 5-6)?

4. Tax collectors were ostracized because they extorted money from fellow Jews for the Roman occupation forces. Why does Jesus risk his reputation by entering Zacchaeus's home (v. 7)?

5. What stereotypes of Jesus might your nonbelieving friends have?

How can you change these stereotypes?

6. What facts does Zacchaeus's formal announcement (v. 8) reveal about him (see also, Leviticus 6:1-5)?

7. What do you imagine Zacchaeus thinks and feels as he hears Jesus say, "Today salvation has come to this house"?

8. What must it mean to Zacchaeus when the King of the kingdom publicly declares him a "son of Abraham" (v. 9)? (How will this change his holiday plans?)

9. Verse 10 holds a surprise! Jesus was seeking as well. What two clues in verse 5 show that Jesus had also heard about Zacchaeus and had come looking for this particular man?

10. How can we avoid making assumptions about whether someone is likely or unlikely to receive Jesus Christ?

How can we find out what they already know and feel about him?

11. In addition to believing the facts about Jesus and repenting, we must receive him as our King. Zacchaeus did that by receiving him into his home. How can we do this today?

Ask the Lord to make you a joyful servant, sensitively and lovingly helping the most unlikely seekers.

Now or Later

Luke 19:10 shows that Jesus is dramatizing the story he had told to tax collectors, probably a few days earlier (Luke 15:4-6). Now the Shepherd has left his ninety-nine safe sheep in order to search for one lost sheep. In our day Jesus still lovingly searches for "lost" people. What do you suppose are some ways he lets them know he is seeking them?

7

Counting the Cost

Jesus is sometimes presented as the ultimate product. He will help our grades go up, our weight go down and our teeth to be as white as can be. It is good to approach people on the basis of their felt needs, but we must also present the cost of being a disciple. People must know who Jesus really is and the demands he makes on his followers.

GROUP DISCUSSION. If you remember a specific conversion experience, how much of the gospel did you understand? Did anyone pressure you to make a decision? Did you face any family opposition? Did anyone help you grow? Talk about your experience.

PERSONAL REFLECTION. How would you evangelize someone from a non-Christian religion, knowing he or she might be disinherited or disowned by family on conversion?

Jesus' last journey to Jerusalem occupies more than half of Luke's Gospel, but our focus is on only one incident and its context. In 9:51 Luke says Jesus "resolutely set out for Jerusalem." It took resolve—crucifixion awaited him. The Jews of tiny Palestine had had ample opportunity to see and hear Jesus. Religious leaders were plotting his death. The air was so politicized that religious decisions had political implications. Many people had turned back from following Jesus, others feared to confess him openly or receive him in their homes. Yet great crowds accompanied him to Passover. He asked the Twelve to pray for more disciples, which makes his words to this holiday crowd surprising. He teaches us an important lesson.

Passover was like a combined religious festival and national independence week. Participation was obligatory for all men who could make the journey, and women and children were welcome. It was a happy time with picnics and singing and friendly chats. *Read Luke 14:25-35.*

1. Look closely at verses 25-26. What information do you discover about the crowd?

2. What would it have been like to be part of this crowd?

3. In the context of the chapter, Jesus uses *becoming a disciple* interchangeably with *receiving eternal life* and *being saved*. Consider Jesus' first condition in verse 26. Since he could not be asking them to *hate* their families, how were they to understand his words (compare with Matthew 15:3-4)?

4. Consider Jesus' second condition in Luke 14:26-27. What is he asking of these men (see also 9:22-26)?

---

5. In verses 28-32 Jesus gives two brief illustrations. What lesson was the crowd supposed to draw about discipleship from the example of the foolish builder?

---

6. If people make premature decisions for Christ and then drop out, how is it likely to affect them and the believers and nonbelievers who know them? From your experience, how are believers and nonbelievers affected when a professing Christian doesn't really follow Jesus?

---

7. How is war a truer picture of Jesus' mission than a building project, and how does it explain his stiff requirements?

---

8. Consider Jesus' third condition in verse 33. How might this have upset their expectations even more than the other two?

---

9. What difference does it make to you that your possessions belong to Christ?

10. How were these followers, who had no genuine commitment to Jesus, like "salt" without saltiness (vv. 34-35)?

11. What are some reasons that Christians might pressure seekers into premature decisions?

How can we responsibly determine if someone understands enough to make a commitment?

12. How can we help seekers make rightly motivated commitments regardless of personal cost?

Ask God to help you evangelize responsibly, helping seekers to count the cost and to mature.

Now or Later

Jesus said, "Make disciples . . . teaching them to obey all that I have commanded you" (Matthew 28:18-20). Reflect on how to "disciple" seekers into the kingdom so they can make intermediate responses to the Lord, at their own pace, as they discover new truth, until they come to full commitment and assurance of salvation. What do you see as some of the key aspects of discipleship?

8

Friendship Evangelism

Many Christians do evangelism like guerrilla warfare. They make occasional raids into enemy territory, get a few "decisions" and then retreat to the safety of their "holy huddles." They spend so much time in a kind of Christian ghetto that they have no genuine friendships elsewhere and are hardly aware of the changing culture around them. Outsiders have little opportunity to see the gospel lived out in these Christians' conduct or to hear it from their lips.

GROUP DISCUSSION. Did any close friend or family member introduce you to Christ? What are some reasons we may find it difficult to evangelize the people who know us best?

PERSONAL REFLECTION. Do you have any close friends who are not convinced Christians? If so, consider how you could share the gospel with them. If not, can you think of someone you might befriend?

Jesus developed friendships with seekers. This glimpse into the beginning of his public ministry provides a model for making friends for the sake of the gospel and winning old friends and family, who are often our biggest challenge.

John the Baptist had been preaching to huge crowds on the banks of the Jordan River, announcing that the Messiah, God's promised King, was about to appear to initiate his kingdom. But only righteous people could enter. Crowds came for baptism to show their unworthiness and their repentance. Then Jesus himself came for baptism! God showed John that this was the long-awaited Messiah. John's helpers heard him say in awe and wonder, "Look, the Lamb of God, who takes away the sin of the world!" In John 1 we read what one of John the Baptist's assistants recalls about the following day. *Read John 1:35-51.*

1. What thoughts and feelings do you think John the Baptist's words aroused in his two disciples mentioned in verse 35?

2. Jesus used a "come and see" approach (vv. 38-39). Why would this be more effective than asserting his deity?

3. How can we help our nonbelieving friends to "come and see" Jesus in action?

4. Even in temporary lodgings Jesus used hospitality evangelism (v. 39). What are some ways we can involve friends so they can "come and see" us live out the gospel?

5. Look at verses 40-42. How would you describe Andrew's thoughts and feelings?

6. As we seek to bring family members or friends to Jesus, why is our attitude toward the good news important?

7. The next day Jesus finds their friend Philip, and Philip finds his friend Nathanael (vv. 43-46). What do you notice about Philip's tactics with Nathanael compared with how Jesus was approaching them all (v. 39)?

8. Nathanael knew the Messiah had to come from Bethlehem, not Nazareth (Micah 5:2). But why do Jesus' words immediately dispel his skepticism (vv. 46-50)?

9. Jesus' first six disciples were relatives and acquaintances from a single fishing village (v. 44). What advantages are there in evangelizing natural groupings of people like families or colleagues at work?

What acquaintances do you have in your workplace, school or neighborhood whose friendship you could begin to cultivate?

10. These men were quickly convinced that Jesus was God's promised King, but it took much longer to confess him as God. Jesus gives them many months. Why is it important not to pressure people too early about making a decision?

---

11. Jesus' "come and see" method is also the most effective way for us to win friends and family. What makes it difficult for us to let them observe our lives?

---

12. The content of the gospel demands to be shared with excitement. If we have taken the gospel for granted, how can we recover the excitement and the wonder of it?

Ask God to help you see the gospel through the eyes of someone who has never heard it before, and then help the people closest to you to grasp it too.

Now or Later

Think about where in your life you could cut down on time spent with believers to make time for seekers (of your own gender). Think of a seeker you might invite over or an activity to do together. Would he or she feel welcome in some fun or work activity with your Christian friends?

9

Talking with Strangers

Most of us are around strangers much of the time—at our workplace, campus, neighborhood, mall, supermarket, hairdresser, doctor's office, coffee shop, baseball game. Some of us have found great opportunities to witness on planes and in airports. But we cannot talk to everyone. How can we know who to approach?

GROUP DISCUSSION. Some people are outgoing and easily converse with strangers everywhere. Others find it difficult to talk to strangers about anything. In every conversation we either assume the role of host or guest. How can it help us to try to be the host?

PERSONAL REFLECTION. How do you personally feel about telling the gospel to strangers?

Philip had been one of seven men in charge of a social assistance program for the early church in Jerusalem. Then his close friend Stephen was stoned, and Philip himself, like many others, became victim of the fierce persecution Saul of Tarsus led against the followers of Jesus. Acts 8:4 says that "those who were scattered preached the word everywhere they went." Philip had already made so many converts in Samaria (probably the capital city—modern Nablus) that Peter and

John came to help. Then Philip went south to the Gaza Road, which linked Jerusalem with Egypt and Ethiopia (Nubia). *Read Acts 8:26-40.*

---

1. What facts can we discover about this traveling stranger before his encounter with Philip?

---

2. Most of us do not receive the kinds of direct guidance described in verses 26 and 29. How might the Holy Spirit indicate to one of us that we should witness to a particular person?

---

3. Picture the highway scene. This African probably rode a luxurious chariot in a caravan of other slowly moving chariots. It was dangerous to travel alone. He may have had a small entourage. Having been guided to the chariot, how does Philip know how to initiate the conversation (vv. 30-31)?

What are some natural ways we might begin talking with a stranger about the gospel?

---

4. To hitch a ride on a hot, desert highway proved beneficial to Philip too. How might the fact that Philip accepted help from this man have played a part in their relationship?

5. What advantage does Philip gain by asking a question and listening to the man before he begins to evangelize?

6. Together in the chariot the two men have one of the first recorded investigative (evangelistic) Bible studies (vv. 32-35). What are some of the advantages of including Bible study discussions as a major part of your evangelism?

7. How can you be prepared to lead spontaneous Bible discussions when occasions arise?

8. Imagine that you are Philip. How might you use the Isaiah passage to begin telling the man the good news about Jesus (vv. 32-35)?

9. What shows that Philip also explained the need for a personal response to Jesus (vv. 36-39)?

Why do you suppose he talked to him about baptism?

10. Circumstances made discipling the man impossible, but what spiritual resources did the man take with him?

_____

11. What could you do to disciple a convert you couldn't see again?

_____

12. Verses 39-40 tells us that the Lord took Philip away and that Philip preached elsewhere. The eunuch "went on his way rejoicing." Looking at the passage as a whole, what principles for talking with strangers might apply to your life?

Ask God to give you courage, wisdom and a sense of urgency to tell the good news to strangers around you.

Now or Later

The next time you walk into a room full of people (a waiting room in an office, airport and so on), try saying a friendly "hello" to everyone in general as you arrive. Often this breaks the ice and encourages someone to ask a question or make small talk. Then insert a comment about God into the middle of your conversation—to fish out a significant question you can then answer.

Assume that your encounters with strangers are no accident but God's planning. God messes with airline computers to delay flights! He messes with our cars so that we have an opportunity talk with a mechanic or tow-truck driver. What examples of this have you seen in your life?

10

Crosscultural Evangelism

Acts 17:16-34

Why consider crosscultural evangelism if you do not plan to live abroad? Two reasons. First, we are surrounded by immigrants, international students, guest workers, refugees, tourists and illegal aliens. God brings them for us to evangelize—he loves them. Second, in our postmodern, pluralist milieu there is no longer a basic social and moral consensus. Absolute truth is rejected and people seek their own "truths" in pantheism, occultism, neopaganism and more. We are splintered into tiny subcultures. New questions are asked.

GROUP DISCUSSION. Of all the people you know, who has the most different cultural background from your own? In what ways are you similar?

PERSONAL REFLECTION. What fairly recent arrivals from other countries do you see the most often in a week? How many do you know by name? Do you think God might have sent them to you?

Our situation is like the first-century Roman Empire. In Acts 17 we find Paul, a trilingual Jewish Christian communicating the gospel to Greek philosophers in Athens, intellectual capital of the ancient world. Luke records three sermons that were typical of Paul's preaching to the three major cultural groups. At a synagogue in Pisidian Antioch, he preaches from the Old Testament to Jews and Gentile God-fearers, and presents Jesus as Messiah (Acts 13). Paul and Barnabas fled persecution and ended up in Lystra. Here were barbarians— not savages but people whose main language was not Greek. After Paul heals a lame man, the priest and people prepare an animal sacrifice in honor of Paul and Barnabas, convinced they are Zeus and Hermes in human form! The apostles do not understand the Lycaonian language and so barely succeed in restraining them. Then Paul tells them the good news of a living God who created everything on earth and in the sea and all that is in them, who has always given the Lycaonians rain and crops, because he wants them to be glad (Acts 14). But what does Paul say to the Greeks—the philosophers of Athens? *Read Acts 17:16-34.*

---

1. Paul, who once again was fleeing persecution, awaits Silas and Timothy in Athens before proceeding to Corinth (v. 16). As a tourist, how does Paul know "the city was *full* of idols?"

What would he have been thinking and feeling at this time?

---

2. Paul begins evangelizing in the synagogue and the marketplace (vv. 17-18). Why do you think he felt these two places were strategic?

---

3. What are some of the common gathering places for nonbelievers in your area, especially those from different ethnic or cultural backgrounds?

4. Why did the idea of Jesus and his resurrection seem so strange to the Athenians?

5. The Areopagus hill—where the chief court in Athens met to try cases—overlooked the city marketplace. Paul was invited to a meeting in session, but he was not on trial (vv. 19-21). As he began his lecture, what common ground did he find with the Athenians (v. 22-23)?

6. Why is it important to find common ground when sharing the gospel crossculturally? (What might have happened if Paul had begun by condemning the Athenians' idolatry?)

7. Paul knew all about their "unknown God"—knew him personally! What stupendous claims does he make for God in verses 24-27?

8. Paul's words to the Athenians were obviously based on Scripture. So why did he quote Greek poetry instead of the Bible (vv. 28-29)?

9. What books, movies or songs might you use constructively in evangelism?

What approach would you take if you were talking to someone of another culture?

---

10. Paul says God had long been patiently overlooking the ignorance of pagan people (vv. 30- 31). What new fact now requires them to repent of their ignorance and idolatry?

---

11. How are the responses to Paul's message typical of people who are hearing the gospel for the first time (vv. 32-34)?

What kinds of things might have brought more positive responses?

Ask God to help you understand enough of other people's beliefs to learn to answer them in ways that will open them to the gospel of Jesus Christ.

Now or Later

In your evangelism you must always discover how seekers under-stand their religion since they may not know any more about it than most Westerners know about Christianity. For more on postmodern-ism, read Timothy Phillips and Dennis Okholm's *Christian Apologetics in the Postmodern World*. For more on non-Christian religions, read Norman Anderson's *Christianity and World Religions*. Can you start to work on a foreign language?

11

Balanced Expectations

Mark 4:1-25

In a series of large outreach meetings in Brazil, about half the people would receive Jesus Christ but few ever came to church. They were willing to receive Jesus as often as you asked. But they had not understood the call for commitment. In contrast in North Africa, friends evangelized for several years without seeing a single conversion. Our personal evangelism can result in a variety of responses. There is no greater joy than helping seekers find God and grow to spiritual maturity. But it is discouraging when we get little response or seekers' "decisions" have not brought them to Christ.

GROUP DISCUSSION. When have you been discouraged by poor response to your efforts toward evangelism? Have you ever seen someone receive Jesus Christ and then fall away? How did it make you feel?

PERSONAL REFLECTION. Are you content with your efforts in evangelism so far? Explain why or why not.

Mark, Matthew and Luke all record this parable, each with slightly differing emphasis and detail. Matthew suggests it was late afternoon after a day of teaching and healing. Mark adds that Jesus and his disciples had been too busy to eat, and his mother and brothers could not get to him through the crowd (Mark 3:20, 31). Yet once again Jesus leaves the house for the nearby lakeside to meet people. Many have heard him before. The religious leaders are hostile and illogically attribute his exorcisms to the devil. If they admit Jesus' power is from God, they stand to lose everything. Jesus knows this audience. From now on he will teach only in parables. *Read Mark 4:1-25.*

1. Imagine you are present in this scene. From verses 1-2, describe everything you might see and hear.

Why would Jesus get into the boat to speak?

2. Consider the parable Jesus tells the audience in verses 3-9. What do you suppose listeners got out of this simple farm story?

3. Jesus' disciples did not understand the parable (v. 13). What would have helped them to find the meaning of Jesus' parables (vv. 10-12)?

4. According to verses 11-12, what seems to be Jesus' reason for using a parable?

5. How do verses 21-25 further clarify Jesus' answer?

What would determine the response of the listeners?

6. In verses 14-20 Jesus is telling this crowd about itself. (With such an audience, no wonder he changed his method!) What four kinds of listeners can we expect in an average group of nonbelievers, whether we are giving a sermon or evangelizing individuals?

7. What keeps the first three kinds of people from listening more carefully?

8. When have you run into some of these kinds of people in your evangelistic efforts?

9. What motivated Jesus to continue teaching these crowds at all?

10. According to the principle in verse 25, what happens to our spiritual discernment each time we respond positively or negatively to God's Word?

11. Personal evangelism is more like planting trees than indiscriminately sowing a large field. Since the condition of the soil matters, what are ways we can improve seekers' receptivity and understanding, and bring them to a genuine commitment?

12. In what ways does Jesus' telling of this parable affect our expectations, and encourage and help us in our evangelism?

Pray for specific nonbelievers you know who seem hardened or indifferent to Jesus Christ.

Now or Later

Consider indifferent or hostile nonbelievers you know and consider whether there is any way you could make them more responsive to Jesus Christ. How might they respond if you could get them to study this passage with you? Tell them you've just been learning some surprising stuff and thought they might be interested too.

12

Facing
Opposition

More Christians are persecuted today than in any previous period of history. Adherents of non-Christian religions feel threatened by the rapidly growing Christian church—now present in every country! In Western cultures, some try to stifle our truth claims, make us privatize our faith and force religious neutrality. But even in politically correct environments we must not allow ourselves to be intimidated but to lovingly share the good news! Anyone who regularly presents the gospel to others will face opposition, whether subtle or overt.

GROUP DISCUSSION. If politically correct enforcers dominate your campus or workplace, you may have been feeling pressure not to mention your faith since it is considered intolerant and judgmental of other people's private "truths." How have you or your Christian friends experienced this kind of opposition?

PERSONAL REFLECTION. How might your life change if Christianity were declared illegal? Would you still share your faith?

Jesus had died, risen, ascended to God's throne and sent the Holy Spirit. Then Peter had preached his remarkable Pentecost sermon, and three thousand men (plus women and children) had joined the tiny Jesus community. Peter and John healed a forty-year-old crippled man at a temple gate (Acts 3) who then followed them into the temple, running and jumping! Word spread all over Jerusalem and huge crowds came. Peter said the man was healed by Jesus, "the Author of life." The priests are desperate to stop this Jesus "superstition." But how do you arrest a ghost? They interrupt Peter's sermon in the temple. *Read Acts 4:1-22.*

1. Set the scene in verses 1-4. What various activities were taking place and who was involved?

2. Why were the Jewish authorities so threatened by what Peter had said and done?

3. Peter and John were being obedient to God in making Jesus Christ known. In your opinion, why didn't God protect them from arrest and trial (v. 3)?

4. How do you think you would have felt if you were on trial before all these religious authorities (vv. 5-7)?

5. How did the priests' question play right into Peter's hands?

6. When Peter began to speak, he was "filled with the Holy Spirit" (v. 8). How did the power of the Spirit show in his words and attitude (vv. 9-13)?

7. What things about Peter and John surprised and astonished these Jewish priests and lawyers, and why (v. 13)?

8. What considerations led these supreme council members to give the men a light sentence (vv. 14-22)?

9. *Read Acts 4:23-31.* How was the evangelism of these early Christians affected by the convictions they express in prayer about God?

their thinking about Jesus?

their use of God's Word?

10. Why do you think the believers pray for boldness rather than freedom from opposition (v. 29)?

How can we distinguish boldness from the tactlessness and brashness that turn people off?

—————————————————————————————————————

11. How can these things help and encourage us when we face opposition in our evangelism?

Ask God to make you skillful and courageous in lifestyle evangelism and to keep you faithful when you encounter opposition here—or if he sends you to a country hostile to Jesus Christ.

Now or Later

—————————————————————————————————————

12. *Read 1 Peter 3:13-16.* In Jerusalem Peter had respectfully disobeyed the religious leaders who knew the truth and rejected it. In Nero's Rome more than thirty years later, he gives surprising instructions to the believers. They must evangelize, but without flaunting their faith before the civil authorities. Slaves (85 percent of the people) were to give good service even to abusive masters, and wives were to win their husbands by loving conduct. What difference would it make for them "to reverence Jesus Christ in their hearts" (RSV)?

—————————————————————————————————————

13. What would their verbal evangelism mainly consist of?

—————————————————————————————————————

14. In situations of persecution, why is it better to get nonbelievers to ask us questions?

Leader's Notes

MY GRACE IS SUFFICIENT FOR YOU. (2 COR 12:9)

Leading a Bible discussion can be an enjoyable and rewarding experience. But it can also be *scary*—especially if you've never done it before. If this is your feeling, you're in good company. When God asked Moses to lead the Israelites out of Egypt, he replied, "O Lord, please send someone else to do it"! (Ex 4:13). It was the same with Solomon, Jeremiah and Timothy, but God helped these people in spite of their weaknesses, and he will help you as well.

You don't need to be an expert on the Bible or a trained teacher to lead a Bible discussion. The idea behind these inductive studies is that the leader guides group members to discover for themselves what the Bible has to say. This method of learning will allow group members to remember much more of what is said than a lecture would.

These studies are designed to be led easily. As a matter of fact, the flow of questions through the passage from observation to interpretation to application is so natural that you may feel that the studies lead themselves. This study guide is also flexible. You can use it with a variety of groups—student, professional, neighborhood or church groups. Each study takes forty-five to sixty minutes in a group setting.

There are some important facts to know about group dynamics and encouraging discussion. The suggestions listed below should enable you to effectively and enjoyably fulfill your role as leader.

Preparing for the Study

1. Ask God to help you understand and apply the passage in your own life. Unless this happens, you will not be prepared to lead others. Pray too for the various members of the group. Ask God to open your hearts to the message of his Word and motivate you to action.

2. Read the introduction to the entire guide to get an overview of the entire book and the issues which will be explored.

3. As you begin each study, read and reread the assigned Bible passage to familiarize yourself with it.

4. This study guide is based on the New International Version of the Bible. It will help you and the group if you use this translation as the basis for your study and discussion.

5. Carefully work through each question in the study. Spend time in meditation and reflection as you consider how to respond.

6. Write your thoughts and responses in the space provided in the study guide. This will help you to express your understanding of the passage clearly.

7. It might help to have a Bible dictionary handy. Use it to look up any unfamiliar words, names or places. (For additional help on how to study a passage, see chapter five of *How to Lead a LifeGuide Bible Study*, InterVarsity Press.)

8. Consider how you can apply the Scripture to your life. Remember that the group will follow your lead in responding to the studies. They will not go any deeper than you do.

9. Once you have finished your own study of the passage, familiarize yourself with the leader's notes for the study you are leading. These are designed to help you in several ways. First, they tell you the purpose the study guide author had in mind when writing the study. Take time to think through how the study questions work together to accomplish that purpose. Second, the notes provide you with additional background information or suggestions on group dynamics for various questions. This information can be useful when people have difficulty understanding or answering a question. Third, the leader's notes can alert you to potential problems you may encounter during the study.

10. If you wish to remind yourself of anything mentioned in the leader's notes, make a note to yourself below that question in the study.

Leading the Study

1. Begin the study on time. Open with prayer, asking God to help the group to understand and apply the passage.

2. Be sure that everyone in your group has a study guide. Encourage the group to prepare beforehand for each discussion by reading the introduction to the guide and by working through the questions in the study.

3. At the beginning of your first time together, explain that these studies are meant to be discussions, not lectures. Encourage the members of the group to participate. However, do not put pressure on those who may be hesitant to speak during the first few sessions. You may want to suggest the following guidelines to your group.

☐ Stick to the topic being discussed.

☐ Your responses should be based on the verses which are the focus of the discussion and not on outside authorities such as commentaries or speakers.

☐ These studies focus on a particular passage of Scripture. Only rarely should you refer to other portions of the Bible. This allows for everyone to participate in in-depth study on equal ground.

☐ Anything said in the group is considered confidential and will not be discussed outside the group unless specific permission is given to do so.

☐ We will listen attentively to each other and provide time for each person present to talk.

☐ We will pray for each other.

4. Have a group member read the introduction at the beginning of the discussion.

5. Every session begins with a group discussion question. The question or activity is meant to be used before the passage is read. The question introduces the theme of the study and encourages group members to begin to open up. Encourage as many members as possible to participate, and be ready to get the discussion going with your own response.

This section is designed to reveal where our thoughts or feelings need to be transformed by Scripture. That is why it is especially important not to read the passage before the discussion question is asked. The passage will tend to color the honest reactions people would otherwise give because they are, of course, supposed to think the way the Bible does.

You may want to supplement the group discussion question with an icebreaker to help people to get comfortable. See the community section of *Small Group Idea Book* for more ideas.

You also might want to use the personal reflection question with your group. Either allow a time of silence for people to respond individually or discuss it together.

6. Have a group member (or members if the passage is long) read aloud the passage to be studied. Then give people several minutes to read the passage again silently so that they can take it all in.

7. Question 1 will generally be an overview question designed to briefly survey the passage. Encourage the group to look at the whole passage, but try to avoid getting sidetracked by questions or issues that will be addressed later in the study.

8. As you ask the questions, keep in mind that they are designed to be used just as they are written. You may simply read them aloud. Or you may prefer to express them in your own words.

There may be times when it is appropriate to deviate from the study guide. For example, a question may have already been answered. If so, move on to the next question. Or someone may raise an important question not covered in the guide. Take time to discuss it, but try to keep the group from going off on tangents.

9. Avoid answering your own questions. If necessary, repeat or rephrase them until they are clearly understood. Or point out something you read in the leader's notes to clarify the context or meaning. An eager group quickly becomes passive and silent if they think the leader will do most of the talking.

10. Don't be afraid of silence. People may need time to think about the question before formulating their answers.

11. Don't be content with just one answer. Ask, "What do the rest of you think?" or "Anything else?" until several people have given answers to the question.

12. Acknowledge all contributions. Try to be affirming whenever possible. Never reject an answer. If it is clearly off-base, ask, "Which verse led you to that conclusion?" or again, "What do the rest of you think?"

13. Don't expect every answer to be addressed to you, even though this will probably happen at first. As group members become more at ease, they will begin to truly interact with each other. This is one sign of healthy discussion.

14. Don't be afraid of controversy. It can be very stimulating. If you don't resolve an issue completely, don't be frustrated. Move on and keep it in mind for later. A subsequent study may solve the problem.

15. Periodically summarize what the group has said about the passage. This helps to draw together the various ideas mentioned and gives continuity to the study. But don't preach.

16. At the end of the Bible discussion you may want to allow group members a time of quiet to work on an idea under "Now or Later." Then discuss what you experienced. Or you may want to encourage group members to work on these ideas between meetings. Give an opportunity during the session for people to talk about what they are learning.

17. Conclude your time together with conversational prayer, adapting the prayer suggestion at the end of the study to your group. Ask for God's help in following through on the commitments you've made.

18. End on time.

Many more suggestions and helps are found in *How to Lead a LifeGuide Bible Study*, which is part of the LifeGuide Bible Study series.

Components of Small Groups

A healthy small group should do more than study the Bible. There are four components to consider as you structure your time together.

Nurture. Small groups help us to grow in our knowledge and love of God. Bible study is the key to making this happen and is the foundation of your small group.

Community. Small groups are a great place to develop deep friendships with other Christians. Allow time for informal interaction before and after each study. Plan activities and games that will help you get to know each other. Spend time having fun together—going on a picnic or cooking dinner together.

Worship and prayer. Your study will be enhanced by spending time praising God together in prayer or song. Pray for each other's needs—and keep track of how God is answering prayer in your group. Ask God to help you to apply what you are learning in your study.

Outreach. Reaching out to others can be a practical way of applying what you are learning, and it will keep your group from becoming self-focused. Host a series of evangelistic discussions for your friends or neighbors. Clean up the yard of an elderly friend. Serve at a soup kitchen together, or spend a day working on a Habitat house.

Many more helps in each of these areas are found in *Small Group Idea Book.* Information on building a small group can be found in *Small Group Leaders' Handbook* and *The Big Book on Small Groups* (both from InterVarsity Press). Reading through one of these books would be worth your time.

Study 1. Why Spread the Good News? Luke 15:1-2, 11-32.
Purpose: To examine our motives for evangelism in light of the Father's amazing love and grace.
Question 1. This passage is a remarkable example of how much can be accomplished through the telling of a good story. We can teach profound theological truths, challenge assumptions, cut through prejudices and touch hearts, all without losing people's attention. We should learn to retell some of Jesus' stories as we share the gospel with those around us.
Question 3. The "distant country" (v. 13) was outside Jewish territory. The Old Testament dietary laws would not permit the Jews to eat pork (Lev 11).
Question 4. For any Jewish boy to be associated with pigs would be shocking and revolting to Jewish listeners, but especially the ultra religious folks Jesus was speaking to. Jesus is deliberately "pressing their religious buttons" with these kind of details.
Question 6. The parable shows that sin is often due to willful choice and a desire for indulgence. Jesus is unrelenting in showing us sin's deception, disillusionment, suffering, slavery and despair.
Question 7. Jesus says that the son "came to his senses." In other words, he finally agreed with God's view of reality. Repentance involved two things: First, the boy's perception of reality was altered from stubbornly insisting on self-rule to bowing to God's rule. Second, repentance involved a willed response. He didn't just think differently, his change of heart manifested itself in definite action.

Two things seemed to help him "come to his senses": disgust and homesickness. He was no doubt appalled by how low he had sunk, and he had the memory of a former time of joy and plenty in his father's home.
Question 8. Many of the parables would have shocked their original audience because they were often designed to overthrow existing values and prejudices. In this case, they expected the father of the story to be harsh and expel the boy for such gross sin, whether he was repentant or not.
Question 9. The description of the son's return and the father's welcome "is as vivid as that of his departure. . . . Because his father saw him 'while he was still a long way off' (v. 20) has led many to assume that the father was waiting for him, perhaps daily searching the distant road hoping for his appearance. . . . The father's 'compassion' assumes some knowledge of the son's pitiable condition, perhaps from reports. Some have pointed out that a father in that

culture would not normally run as he did, which, along with his warm embrace and kissing, adds to the impact of the story. Clearly Jesus used every literary means to heighten the contrast between the father's attitude and that of the elder brother (and of the Pharisees, cf. vv. 1-2). . . .

"The robe was a ceremonial one such as a guest of honor would be given, the ring signified authority, and the sandals were those only a free man would wear" (Walter L. Liefeld, *Luke*, in *The Expositor's Bible Commentary*, ed. Frank E. Gaebelein [Grand Rapids, Mich.: Zondervan, 1976], 8:984).

Question 10. Sometimes we are motivated to share the gospel for the wrong reasons: guilt, duty, a sense of superiority and so on. We share the good news because someone very precious and of immense worth to God is lost and God is seeking to find them.

Questions 11-12. The elder son's words describe the self-righteousness of some Pharisees who criticized Jesus. The father's words indicate the possibilities which the elder son (or Pharisees) had never appreciated and the privileges he had never enjoyed. The elder son could have always enjoyed the grace and love of God. Instead religion had been an activity of rites and duties done from a sense of burden rather than a joyful heart. Instead of being grateful that God had pardoned his own sin and living in intimate relationship and devotion to his father, he obeyed his father's command out of a weary joylessness.

Study 2. A Life That Speaks. Colossians 3:5—4:6.

Purpose: To see how people are drawn to the gospel because of what Christ is doing in us.

Question 1. The group should find all the sins, but you won't have time to discuss them. Temple prostitution made immorality acceptable for men. Idolatry permeated everything—even eating in a restaurant or shopping for groceries! Pagans called Christians antisocial for avoiding so many activities. Christ in them would powerfully transform their lives (Eph 3:20-21).

Question 3. Have the group find all the spiritual qualities in this passage, but there will not be time to discuss them all.

These qualities will have an impact at unexpected moments: When we show patience when others would lose their temper. Or show humility when criticized or insulted. Or show compassion where others express disdain. Or we show little kindnesses, without any reason, making "the most of every opportunity" (Col 4:6).

Question 4. Galatians 3:28 specifies that male and female are equal in Christ.

Question 5. They all had Jesus Christ living in them! They all belonged to the same "body." The church is primarily an *organism*, not an organization. Slaves and masters, males and females were equal. "Greek or Jew" referred to nationality; "circumcision" to Gentile proselyte and Jewish converts who kept Jewish ceremonial and dietary laws. "Barbarians" were not savages but people whose first language was not Greek. Many prisoners of war were sold in the slave markets, and "Scythians" referred to all foreigners. In Christ, racial, social, gender, economic and educational differences made no difference. **Question 6.** People today are open to the supernatural but want evidences. The best "power encounter" is not healings and exorcisms. Dr. Francis Schaeffer said the two most powerful evidences for the gospel are a godly life and a loving Christian fellowship, because they are the only two "miracles" the devil cannot counterfeit. Jesus said it in John 13:34-35. You must have a minimum of two Christians to display Christian love and trust. Involve other Christians in your workplace, campus or neighborhood to evangelize with you.

Question 7. Thankfulness makes us aware of the Lord's presence in us, eliminates negative feelings like fear and lethargy, fills us with faith and courage, and turns all our tasks into worship! Fulfillment in secular work does not come from the job but from what we bring to it.

Question 8. Spouses were to submit to each other (Eph 5:21). The culture required the wife's submission, but Paul turned it into a whole new ball game! Now the husband had to *love* his wife as much as Christ loved the church (Eph 5:25)! The wife could now submit, not because of his demand but voluntarily, out of love for him, love for the Lord and her concern for Christian testimony. Don't get bogged down on a discussion of women's role today—a different question which requires further biblical study.

The householder (father) now had to be gentle with his children so they could obey out of love, and he was to give them spiritual instruction (Eph 6:1-4). In our society of dysfunctional families, the testimony of a Christian family is great, even when imperfect.

Question 9. Don't get bogged down on a discussion of slavery. For Christians, Paul took the slavery out of slavery (1 Cor 7:20-24). He couldn't confront the issue head-on in a totalitarian society. It was against the law for masters to free slaves, because there was a very limited job market. The freed slaves would become vagrants with no social identity. Some masters set their slaves up in business to remain in the household as free partners or clients, even if based in a different city. (Colossians 4:7 and Philemon show Paul sending one runaway slave back to his Christian master.) In our enemy-occupied world, God deals with people realistically, whatever their imperfect milieu. Then he gradually changes it from within through his changed people. As the early church grew, it did eliminate slavery in the empire!

Question 10. Seekers will ask about your faith. Conduct and speech are both necessary—like wings of a jet. Your answers lead to longer conversations. This lifestyle evangelism may impact strangers, but it is essential for people we see frequently. Outsiders were Gentile nonbelievers (1 Cor 14:16-25). *Wise* conduct? Is Paul thinking about Daniel 12:3? "Those who are wise will shine like the brightness of the heavens, and those who lead many to righ-

teousness, like the stars for ever and ever."
Question 11. When we wait for nonbelievers to ask significant questions: (1) We know who to evangelize. (2) They *want* to talk—we are not imposing. (3) The timing is right—they chose it. (4) Their questions show us what to say. We discover truths they believe, truths they lack, their spiritual history, felt needs, hangups and more. (5) We can sensitively cooperate with what the Holy Spirit is already doing in them. (6) We can avoid alienating the indifferent or hostile so our caring lifestyle can turn them into seekers. John Stott says, "We have no liberty to barge unceremoniously into people's privacy or tread clumsily on their corns."(*The Message of 2 Timothy* [Downers Grove, Ill.: InterVarsity Press, 1973], p. 107).

Study 3. Getting People Interested. John 4:4-30.

Purpose: To consider what Jesus' encounter with the woman at the well can teach us about arousing people's interest in the gospel.
Question 1. Women usually drew water in the morning or evening. This woman may have come at noon to avoid contact with others since she was a social outcast.
Question 2. Samaritans were hated by the Jews because they were considered racially and religiously impure. Most pious Jews would walk around Samaria, even though this took them out of their way, in order to avoid contact with this despised people. (*Samaria* referred not only to the capital city but also to the surrounding territory.) Notice that verse 4 states that Jesus believed he "had to go through Samaria."
Question 3. Jesus realizes that people are influenced by not just what they *hear* but what they *see*. By being willing to drink out of the woman's cup, Jesus establishes trust and arouses curiosity.
Question 4. First, the Jews spoke of running water as "living water." It was preferred over still or stagnant water. Of course Jesus is speaking about the water of that is so much more desirable than flat cisterns; while the woman is thinking of flowing water. He uses this phrase in part because he is trying to arouse her curiosity so she will ask more questions. By merely using Christian jargon ("salvation," "sin," "grace"), we can fail to communicate clearly and fail to arouse people's interest
Question 5. Jesus is seeking to arouse her curiosity, but he is not trying to manipulate her into a conversion. If he had given her the "living water" when she asked, then it would have been manipulative because she clearly didn't understand what Jesus was offering. Instead he addresses her deeper needs to help her see that what he is offering is the only thing that can truly satisfy the thirst in her life. If you want to draw out this point, you might ask, "How does Jesus' invitation to go call her husband reveal the difference between persuasion and manipulation?"

Question 6. Raymond E. Brown writes that the "living water" Jesus spoke of probably referred to two things: Jesus' revelation or teaching and the Holy Spirit communicated by Jesus (*The Gospel According to John*, [Garden City, N.Y.: Doubleday, 1966], p. 178).

Question 7. While intellectual questions about the faith are valid and need serious answers, we must not stop there. Christianity also meets our deepest physical, social and emotional needs. These empty places in our lives, where we have used substitute idols to meet our needs, may be the very place where we are most open to God.

Question 8. Around 400 B.C. the Samaritans built a rival temple on Mount Gerizim that the Jews burned in 128 B.C. Evidently the woman was attempting to steer the conversation away from herself to a topic of controversy.

Question 9. Jesus is demonstrating an important aspect of evangelism. First he "cultivates the soil" by arousing her curiosity. Then when he senses she is ready he "plants the seed" by revealing who he is. It is even possible that the third stage of the process of evangelism was accomplished by "reaping the harvest"; although the text doesn't confirm that she was indeed converted.

Question 10. One indication of her excitement is seen in how the woman's opinion of Jesus changes. First, she refers to him as "a Jew" (v. 9), then as a "prophet" (v. 29), then (in a question) as "the Christ" (v. 29). She also comes at an unusual hour to draw water presumably to avoid people she may feel judged by. But after encountering Jesus she has a new kind of transparency. The fact that she left her water jar "seems to be John's way of emphasizing that such a jar would be useless for the type of living water that Jesus has interested her in" (Raymond E. Brown, *Gospel According to John*, p. 173).

Study 4. The Good News. Acts 10:23-48.

Purpose: To become familiar with the content of the gospel and why it is such good news.

Question 1. Cornelius was a centurion who commanded one hundred men of the Italian band. He was a Gentile, but a very devout one. Probably he was a proselyte who believed in the God of Judaism and his government, but had evidently not taken the steps to become a full-fledged proselyte. He was a generous and prayerful man (vs 2). He was not yet a saved man (11:14) even though he was very religious.

Question 2. Cornelius's eagerness and excitement are understandable. It isn't every day that a divinely announced messenger from God visits our home! Angels have become popular again as postmoderns reject the excessive rationalism of the modernist period. But angels are neither little cherubs nor beautiful women. At death no one becomes an angel only to hover around loved ones. Angels are big, powerful, genderless, intelligent, free-willed, holy beings existing in several orders and countless numbers. All were created by

God to serve him. Angels are usually not perceived by our five senses but have on rare occasions appeared visibly to believers (Heb 1—2; Gen 18). Satan, a fallen archangel, led a revolt of evil angels, who war against God and his people for control of the world.

Question 3. Jewish religion would not allow a Jew to enter the home of a Gentile, because they were considered "unclean." For further information on what changed Peter's attitude toward the Gentiles, read verses 9-23.

Question 4. Now we see why a religious and prayerful man liked Cornelius needed to repent, believe in Jesus and be filled with the Holy Spirit. Even a godly man like Peter, absolutely devoted to Jesus and full of the Holy Spirit, could get it wrong. Because of Peter's cultural and religious background, he needed three repeated visions from the Lord before he understood that he was to "call no man unclean." Obeying Jesus and walking in the Spirit is a process of learning how to submit every area of our lives to God's purposes and ways. For Peter it meant that the gospel of Jesus transcends all human barriers. The gospel is a message of reconciliation not only to God but to our neighbor as well.

Question 5. Jesus' life, death and resurrection constituted the gospel for he was Lord, Judge and Savior of all who believe. When Peter states that "God anointed Jesus of Nazareth with the Holy Spirit" (v. 38), he is claiming that Jesus is the Messiah (the anointed one).

Question 7. Peter hints that behind the human execution was a divine plan. And as John Stott writes: "Peter was under no necessity to call the cross 'a tree'; he did it by design in order to indicate that Jesus was bearing in our place the 'curse' or judgment of God on our sins" (*The Spirit, the Church & the World* [Downers Grove, Ill.: InterVarsity Press, 1990], p. 191).

Question 8. Peter is saying that God deliberately caused the risen Christ to be seen by eyewitnesses. This was something that could be verified.

Question 9. Judgment is not a theme we hear discussed today, but Peter makes it clear all will be included; none can escape. Yet judgment need not be a fearful thing since Jesus is the one who bestows salvation, and Peter tells us that "everyone who believes in him receives forgiveness of sins through his name" (Acts 10:43). But the salvation Jesus offers is meaningless to most people until they realize what he has saved them from.

Question 10. J. I. Packer states that belief in Jesus expresses "the idea of a movement of trust going out to, and laying hold of, and resting upon, the object of its confidence" (*God's Words* [Downers Grove, Ill.: InterVarsity Press, 1981], p. 130). We trust Jesus to do for us what we cannot do for ourselves.

Question 11. The gift of the Holy Spirit that God bestowed on Cornelius and his household was the proof Peter (and later the Jerusalem church) needed that God had welcomed believing Gentiles into his family on equal terms with believing Jews. Any Jewish racial or religious prejudice had to be dealt a hammer blow in light of this evidence. And so they glorified God, who "has granted even the Gentiles repentance unto life" (Acts 11:18).

Study 5. Creative Communication. Luke 10:25-37.

Purpose: To teach us how to communicate the gospel more creatively.

Question 1. Notice that the lawyer, obviously very confident in his knowledge of the Old Testament, was testing Jesus. He may have assumed Jesus would prescribe some new rites or ceremonies that would disparage the law. He no doubt came prepared to defeat Jesus in debate. You may also want to ask, "Why do you think the expert in the law wanted to test Jesus" (v. 25)?

Question 3. The lawyer asks, "What must I do to inherit eternal life?" The question seems to assume that he must earn eternal life. Yet when Jesus refers him back to the law, he answers accurately that the issue is not a matter of action but of the heart. Our chief end is to love God wholly. The evidence of our love for God is seen in how we love our neighbor. However even though the lawyer answers correctly it becomes apparent that he is still confused.

Question 4. The lawyer seems to still think that eternal life is earned rather than received through a love relationship with God. He doesn't want to admit he has not lived up to the demands of the law. "The question *Who is my neighbor?* is really an attempt to limit who one's neighbor might be" (Darrell L. Bock, *Luke* [Downers Grove, Ill.: InterVarsity Press, 1994], p. 197).

The lawyer "correctly" understood what the law said about eternal life (Deut 5:5; Lev 19:18), but his answer should not be seen as a definition of the gospel. If we could love God and our neighbor in the way that the law commands, then eternal life would be our reward. But we have not kept these laws; therefore, the law condemns us and leads us to Christ, who offers us eternal life as a free gift (Rom 3:23-24; Gal 3:24).

Question 5. Walter Liefeld offers some geographical information that helps us understand the setting of the parable. "The distance from Jerusalem to Jericho is about seventeen miles, descending sharply toward the Jordan River just north of the Dead Sea. The old road, even more than the present one, curved through rugged, bleak, rocky terrain where robbers could easily hide. It was considered dangerous, even in a day when travel was normally full of hazards" (*Luke*, p. 943).

In our day the name *Samaritan* has positive connotations because of this parable. However, it should be remembered that in Jesus' day Samaritans were despised by the Jews. The original hearers would have been shocked that a Samaritan was the hero of the story. In fact, when Jesus asked, "Which of these three do you think was a neighbor to the man who fell into the hands of robbers?" (v. 36), the "expert in the law" couldn't bring himself to say "the Samaritan," referring instead to "the one who had mercy on him."

Question 6. Verse 31 states that the priest was "going down the same road" (to Jericho). Therefore, he was not on his way to serve at the temple in Jerusalem as is sometimes supposed.

Question 8. Evangelism involves more than just meeting a person's spiritual needs. True evangelism shows compassion and concern for every aspect of the seeker's life.

Question 9. If this question doesn't elicit a response, then you might ask, "Why didn't Jesus simply tell him that no one can truly love one's neighbor as the Law requires?" The lawyer had asked, "Who is my neighbor?" Evidently, his own restricted definition of "neighbor" allowed him to limit his loving acts to those who fit his definition. Everyone else was outside his sphere of responsibility—or so he thought. Jesus' parable shatters this faulty thinking. The Samaritan was a neighbor even though he was a member of a race that was despised by the Jews. He also fulfilled what the law required in a way that far surpassed those who were at the pinnacle of Jewish religion.

Question 10. Jesus may have taken this approach because he knew this man was proud, especially in his confidence that he could fulfill the law's requirements. He needed to see that he couldn't fulfill the law's demands no matter how hard he tried. Such a discovery would most likely make him more humble and possibly more open to seeing his need for Jesus. In his next conversation with Jesus he might say, "I want to love my neighbor, I really do. But I lack the power to love consistently. I do it when it's convenient. God's commands are not only difficult—they're impossible!" Of course that is true when the power source is human and not divine. First, we must let Jesus fill us with his love and strength, and then we are able to serve others.

Study 6. An Unlikely Seeker. Luke 19:1-11.

Purpose: To do thorough evangelism, verifying not only right belief and repentance but helping seekers receive Jesus as their King.

Question 1. All the tax collector passages in Luke—chapters 3, 5, 7, 15, 18, 19—are connected as though they were one chapter, and we need them to understand the Zacchaeus story. He had been hired by Rome because he promised big collections. He would retain employees to squeeze the money out of fellow Jews. He and his subordinates lived lavishly on the excess amounts they extorted. There were poll taxes based on the census, property and business taxes, and duties on goods that crossed internal borders and on goods from the East that crossed the border from Nabataea, the neighboring wealthy puppet kingdom. The collectors took an average forty percent of a citizen's worth!

Jericho was seventy feet below sea level on a fertile plain near the Dead Sea—an international crossroads. Many of Israel's wealthiest people, including a third of the priests, lived in Jericho. It was filled with mansions, and Zacchaeus owned one. But the atmosphere was highly politicized, and most of the crowds passing through sympathized with the revolutionary bands that roamed the countryside. Tax collectors were collaborators with imperialist

Rome—traitors unwelcome in the temple and the synagogues.

Question 2. Verses 3-4 show that Zacchaeus resorted to the undignified climb into the leafy sycamore tree only after his short stature foiled his other attempts. Luke links this story with the healing of the blind man minutes before as two examples of outcasts desperate to meet Jesus—a poor blind beggar and a poor rich man. These are two stories in Luke's series regarding who gets into the kingdom and what is an adequate or inadequate response to Jesus. Zacchaeus had become convinced Jesus was God's King and would set up his kingdom in Jerusalem, but he himself was on the wrong side and left out. Luke expects us to understand that he had heard about Jesus through the industry grapevine. John had baptized many of them. Jesus chose Levi/Matthew as a disciple who puts on an evangelistic banquet for tax-collector friends. Jesus repeatedly ate and drank with tax collectors and other outcasts, which gave Zacchaeus hope (study one).

Question 4. The crowd followed Jesus to the door incredulous that he would go inside! The hero of the separatist majority was consorting with the enemy. No priest or rabbi would have defiled himself by entering and eating in the house of such a man. Some in the crowd were turning against him. They will have him as king over them (19:27) only if he meets their expectations. He wants to disillusion them. He has told them he will not set up a literal kingdom now. First he must die and rise.

Question 5. Correct people's wrong stereotypes of Jesus with Scripture and your personal testimony. Lend books. Get them into a Bible study group.

Question 6. Zacchaeus's gift to the poor shows he now feels guilty but also compassionate toward people he helped impoverish. His 400 percent restitution where the law required only 120 percent shows the depth of his repentance (Num 5:5-7, imagine delving into old accounts!) That he can give so much shows how obscenely rich this Mafia type had become. (They would lend money at exorbitant interest to people who couldn't pay.)

Note that the verbs *give* and *pay back* are both present tense in the Greek. Is it not unthinkable that Zacchaeus would continue defrauding people once he was convinced Jesus was the King? Surely, if he had not already begun his restitution, he would have been ashamed or afraid to meet Jesus.

Question 7. Zacchaeus must have been beside himself with joy! These words could suggest to some that a generous gift to charity, or moral reform, could buy you salvation and a place in the kingdom. Luke's series of narratives on responses to Jesus quash those ideas. Believing the facts about Jesus and genuine repentance were necessary steps, but neither one can ever save anyone! Many people believed in Jesus but failed to follow him out of fear or unwillingness to pay the cost. ("Even the demons believe that—and shudder," James 2:19). The glorious new fact in Zacchaeus' life that day was his personal encounter with Jesus. He had received Jesus into his home and heart to be the King of his life! That was what saved him (Jn 1:12; 1 Jn 5:11-12).

Question 8. Abraham was the great man of faith and founder of the Old Testament people of God for whom the promises were given. Zacchaeus was now a man of faith with full citizenship rights in the kingdom by decree of the King (Lk 13:28-29; Gal 3:7, 9). He could even accompany the King to Passover! (John the Baptist had told Jews that physical descent from Abraham could not save them, Lk 3:7-24.)

Question 9. Jesus already knew Zacchaeus's name! "I must stay at your place today" shows he had been counting on him for lodging. He invited himself confidently into his house because he knew about the man's faith and repentance. Luke expects us to understand that he heard by the same tax-collector grapevine. Jesus knew one mansion in Jericho would have no guests at all. And it was big enough to accommodate his whole team! The last lap of the journey was a whole day's steep climb. "Son of man," from Isaiah and Daniel 7:13-14, was Jesus' favorite term for himself.

Question 10. No one would have guessed that Saul, the persecutor of the church, would ever receive Jesus, but on the Damascus Road he was already under great conviction because of the testimonies of his victims.

Question 11. Seekers must believe the facts, repent and receive Jesus to be King over them, their relationships, activities and possessions. In Revelation 3:20-21 Jesus speaks of each person as a house whose door can be opened only from the inside. *Sins* are only symptoms of *sin*—our terminal disease because we are cut off from God, the only source of life. This is what we must repent of. Sins do not have to be confessed before conversion, but afterward it is good to ask forgiveness where we can.

Now or Later. Talk with seekers about the ways Jesus gently turns our thoughts to him and to ultimate questions. God gives good gifts (Rom 2:4), allows problems, speaks through books, movies, music, TV news, the conduct and words of Christians. Some seekers begin to see God's hand in all that happens around them and soon respond to him.

Study 7. Counting the Cost. Luke 14:25-35.

Purpose: To learn why Jesus wants us to urge seekers to make costly commitments.

Question 1. Jesus' journey wasn't just to Jerusalem but to heaven via Jerusalem. It began in 9:51, and Luke makes fourteen references to its progress. That Jesus had to turn to speak to the crowds shows they considered themselves disciples. No disciple would walk ahead of his rabbi, much less ahead of his king. The omission of husbands might suggest Jesus had lower standards for women, but that is not so. It shows the crowd is made up of men.

Question 2. Verse 11 explains the excitement of the crowds. Jewish people who believed Jesus was God's promised king expected a literal fulfillment of prophecy. Jesus would use supernatural power to free their ancestral lands from Rome and oust the Gentiles. The Jews would get their lands and cities and everyone would be rich. The story had spread that at this Passover Jesus would host his great inaugural banquet. Jesus' parables did not succeed in squelching the rumors. Jesus said his kingdom was like a tiny mustard seed that would become a tree and fill the world. It would be glorious beyond belief because God didn't promise Abraham a tiny piece of Palestine but the whole world! (Rom 4:13). But first Jesus must die and rise, winning the victory over human and cosmic enemies. Then a planet full of rebels must be persuaded into the kingdom. There would be persecution. Jesus could not let people follow on false premises.

Question 3. "Hate" is hyperbole—a deliberate exaggeration for emphasis. They would have to make difficult choices. In Luke 9:59-62 Jesus turned down two volunteers. One asked to wait until he had buried his father. Jesus would have waited for a funeral, but the father's death was not imminent. The volunteer didn't want to rock the boat at home and lose his inheritance. The other one promised to follow but then asked to consult his family. Neither had sufficient commitment. When seekers find God, they should be especially loving to their families, to win them too. But if a choice has to be made, Jesus must take precedence over family. This is a particularly difficult issue for those whose families belong to non-Christian religions. A woman in Spain said she learned that to "hate" one's family in this way can be the best way to love them. Her husband and grown sons had mistreated her, until her costly commitment brought them all to Christ.

Question 4. Armed bands of Jewish revolutionaries roamed Palestine seeking freedom from Rome. The men Jesus addresses would have seen Jewish activists hung on Roman crosses. In a few weeks Jewish authorities would crucify Jesus for sedition, so his followers were in danger (Lk 10:3; 12:4-11). In the next forty years Palestine would become increasingly ungovernable until A.D. 70 when the Roman military destroyed the temple and the city.

Question 5. Both stories were almost certainly from current events. Both the foolish builder and the foolish king were Herod Antipas, who had beheaded John the Baptist a year or two earlier. Now Jesus and the crowds were in Peraea, Herod's territory. Messengers had just come warning Jesus to flee because Herod sought to kill him (13:31). Jesus referred to him as "that fox." He knew Herod could not kill him because his death had to occur in Jerusalem. They were probably passing by the ruins of a pretentious tower the king had never been able to finish—an object of ridicule. The crowds may have laughed appreciatively at Jesus' reference to Herod's folly.

Question 7. Herod had committed a more serious folly. The Jewish people resented fighting his personal war with the powerful puppet-king of Nabataea, whose daughter Herod divorced in order to marry his brother Philip's wife. To provoke a war could leave no option but surrender—on the other king's terms.

All through Luke, Jesus is shown to be the powerful King. He wants people to ask themselves if they can afford not to pay the cost (see Leon Morris, *Luke* [Grand Rapids, Mich.: Eerdmans, 1974] p. 286). Jesus had said it before (Lk 9:21-27). History is a cosmic war for control of this world. Although Jesus has now won the decisive battle on the cross (Col 3:13-15), his lands must now be occupied, and the rebels lovingly persuaded to make an unconditional surrender to the only rightful King.

Question 8. They hoped for wealth: worth a little sacrifice. But now they were to give that up too. The RSV says "renounce." They did not have to give everything away but to give up their right to ownership. "God gives us richly all things to enjoy" (1 Tim 6:17), but they are on loan to us. The only concept of kingship was totalitarian. Jesus used his royal prerogative when he asked to use Peter's boat, a friend's donkey, an upper room. We should not ask how much to give but how much we may use of what God entrusts to us (see Lk 18:28-30).

God gives us salvation by grace. Some in your group may insist that it must therefore be unconditional, a common idea in evangelical circles. It is completely free, never bought or earned, but it is not unconditional. If we enter into this wonderful, freely offered relationship, there are expectations on both sides—like marriage. Total commitment to Christ would seem unreasonable, except that he loves us more than we can love ourselves. Submission brings freedom that can be found no other way (Jn 8:32-36).

Question 11. Christians may press for premature decision for a variety of reasons: poor understanding of salvation, thinking a decision is a conversion, fearing they will lose the "fish," lacking trust in the Holy Spirit or measuring success by large numbers of converts. Methods which ask for a decision after a brief summary of the gospel may win a few partially evangelized seekers, but will harm the majority.

Question 12. The most popular evangelism today is human-centered. God's love is emphasized, but not his holiness. People don't just need a bandage on a few personal inadequacies. They are spiritually dead, and only divine intervention can give them life (Jn 5:24). The pervasive health-and-wealth "prosperity gospel" has no basis in the Bible. To urge quick decisions cheapens the gospel and makes people feel God should be pleased to get their vote. Human-centered evangelism produces a few new births and huge numbers of spiritual stillbirths and miscarriages. Turn the tables. Teach God's holiness as well as his love—two sides of the same coin. Present Jesus Christ so they are filled with awe. Let them worry whether he will accept them. The point is not that God has a wonderful plan for your life but that he has a wonderful plan for this world (Rom 8:18-25)! God owes us nothing at all, but out of mercy and love he offers to indwell us to make us alive forever. He invites us to cooperate with him on his glorious purpose for human history (Eph 1). Try to disciple seekers into the kingdom in a Bible study group. Help them make a firm commitment. Provide the follow-up care every newborn needs.

Study 8. Friendship Evangelism. John 1:35-51.
Purpose: To learn how to share the gospel with our friends and family.
Question 1. John preached the imminent coming of the kingdom of God. The people expected a literal fulfillment of prophecy. Messiah would free them from Rome and rule an earthly kingdom from Jerusalem. But the fulfillment God intended far exceeded their wildest imagination! First, Jesus would have to die and rise, paying for people's sins and giving them eternal life because the animal sacrifices they had offered for years could not do that. Up to that time God had saved believers "on credit." Now God's Lamb would pay that debt. Our salvation and God's reputation were at stake.

These two disciples the Baptist can't bear to lose contact. They request Jesus' address, but what is it they are really asking? How can we learn to see behind seekers' surface questions?

The eyewitness nature of this account indicates that John the Baptist's other helper, along with Andrew, was John, who later wrote this Gospel.
Question 2. The men in the Baptist's inner circle would have been fanatically monotheistic. They could never accept Jesus' claim to deity. That would be a crime punishable by death. Not till near the end of Jesus' ministry does Peter dare say the words aloud (Mt 16)! Jesus' deity was the inevitable conclusion of Jesus' "come and see" method.
Question 3. We can use the "moving pictures" in the Gospels to help our friends observe and interact vicariously with Jesus through the characters, until they reach the same conclusion: Jesus is the Lord of all.
Question 5. Andrew brought his brother Peter, and Mark 1:19 indicates John brought his brother, James. John was always reluctant to mention himself. These four were with Jesus from the start.
Question 8. In verse 50 Jesus alludes to Jacob's dream (Gen 28:10-22). He saw a stairway from earth to heaven with angels going up and down. He awoke and exclaimed, "How awesome is this place! This is none other than the house of God—the gate of heaven." Jesus was *the way* that could lead Nathanael to God. John has grouped narratives to show Jesus' prophetic insight into Andrew and John's motivation, Simon's potential, Nathanael's meditation, Nicodemus's real question, and the Samaritan woman's moral history. In his incarnation Jesus laid aside his divine prerogatives, but on occasion he used the insight and power of a prophet.
Question 9. You can get a chain reaction, and new believers can help each other. Most of a freshman class in one university found God! Sometimes whole families come to faith together.
Question 10. A "new birth" is more a process than a single encounter. Before

they make a firm commitment and gain full assurance of salvation, seekers make a number of intermediate responses to Christ. Most must hear the gospel several times. An expert says a Muslim may need to hear it one hundred times! Be sure seekers have understood before you ask for a decision.

Question 11. We cannot do friendship evangelism with many people at once because it takes time to share our lives with several people. Jesus invited these six disciples to travel with him on and off before they became full disciples. He was often a guest in Peter's house, getting to know his wife, mother-in-law and children. The six met Jesus' mother at a family wedding. They could see his relationship with his brothers who did not believe in him. He went to the fishermen's wharf and accompanied the men in their trawlers. He took them to a banquet, a mountainside retreat, a funeral and to the synagogue. Lifestyle is the most natural and effective way to evangelize.

Study 9. Talking with Strangers. Acts 8:26-40.

Purpose: To learn responsible "encounter evangelism" with strangers met casually.

Question 1. Look for nationality, race, social position, marital status, education, religion and so on.

The kingdom of Ethiopia included part of modern Sudan—from the upper Nile to Khartoum. Candace would have been the queen mother, responsible for all the secular duties of the king because he was considered too sacred to do them. "Eunuchs were commonly employed as court officials in eastern lands from antiquity until quite recent times. . . . This man had visited Jerusalem as a worshiper, perhaps at the time of one of the great pilgrimage-festivals, and was now beguiling his homeward journey by studying a scroll of the book of Isaiah in the Greek version" (F. F. Bruce, *Acts* Grand Rapids, Mich.: Eerdmans, 1968 p. 187).

Synagogues were all over North Africa, and Jewish monotheism was attractive to the educated who no longer believed in the gods. Some became proselytes but most became God-fearers, adhering to Judaism but without the dietary and ceremonial laws. That the eunuch made the long journey, bought the costly handwritten scroll and was reading it already indicate a great spiritual hunger. Was his experience with Judaism in Jerusalem disappointing?

Question 2. Even the apostle Paul did not usually receive such direct guidance (Acts 16). But to find seekers among strangers, always assume that your encounters and seating may have been planned by God. Be friendly. Insert a casual, fitting comment about God into your conversation and watch for clues: Is anyone around you friendly, helpful or needing help, sad, afraid, or extra happy? Does anyone have a book or magazine article you can comment on or ask about? If there is no nibble, try another kind of bait. But relax. You need not force a conversation. The Spirit can guide you to the hungry.

Question 3. Philip uses his head—and his ears and eyes. As he runs alongside, he hears the man read aloud and recognizes the familiar Isaiah passage. He tactfully gets himself invited into the chariot. It is best to say or do something that will get seekers to ask questions so you know they are willing to talk and that you are not invading their privacy or imposing.

Question 4. Accepting some help from a seeker, as well as giving it, helps us avoid paternalism. (But we are not endorsing hitchhiking!)

Question 5. He discovers the seeker's concerns and questions. The man did not even know that the passage speaks of Jesus, so that was the place to begin. Good evangelism is always custom-made. Ask questions and listen.

Question 6. An investigative Bible study is a way to help seekers learn about Jesus through group discussion, usually on a narrative passage of the Bible. As seekers watch Jesus in action, they interact with him vicariously through the characters in the narratives. In fact, the interaction is direct because Jesus is as present in the study group as if he were seated in one of the chairs. He notes the seekers' reactions to himself, opens their minds, warms their hearts and lovingly draws them to himself. For an effective study see Leighton Ford's LifeGuide® Bible Study *Meeting Jesus*.

Question 7. Only a few question-based study guides are designed especially for seekers but some are in several languages. You might want to have a couple of them on hand. *Passport to the Bible* is a great resource for those with no biblical background.

Question 8. Encourage the group to stick to the verses from Isaiah in this passage. If you go back to Isaiah 53, you may not have time to finish the study! Philip *began* with this passage of the innocent sufferer, but mainly he spoke about Jesus—his life, death and resurrection.

Questions 9. Verse 37 reads, "Philip said, 'If you believe with all your heart, you may.' The official answered, 'I believe that Jesus Christ is the Son of God.'" This bit of dialogue is a good idea and it probably occurred, but it is not in the earliest manuscripts, so the NIV and most recent translations put it in a footnote. Throughout the book of Acts, converts were encouraged to be baptized as an expression of their new faith in Christ (Acts 2:38; 8:12, 36-38; 9:18; 10:47-48; 16:15, 33; 19:5). We too should urge new converts to be baptized as part of our follow-up (Mt 28:19) and to join a church (Heb 10:24, 25). But almost certainly there was none in Nubia at this time. (Soon, missionaries filled North Africa with churches!) Even in this wilderness there would have been pools along the way. F. F. Bruce suggests that the two men came to Wadi el-Hesi, northeast of Gaza (*Acts*, p. 189).

Question 10. Isaiah is full of beautiful passages to nourish this African man's spirit and which he could now interpret in terms of Jesus. Philip would pray for him. The man probably won others in Nubia and started a fellowship that could learn together and help each other. Most important, he had Christ living in him through his Spirit, and Christ would never leave him. The One who cared so much about this seeker that he sent Philip to him would surely continue to care for him (Acts 20:32; Jn 14:26).

Question 11. Today we can phone, fax, e-mail, write letters, send books and videos, refer them to Christians in their town and so on. Most important, we can pray for them!

Question 12. Philip wasted no time but started evangelizing the cities of the coastal plain. Then he settled down in Caesarea for urban evangelism. In time, Philip had four unmarried daughters doing ministry. And twenty years later, guess who came to dinner? Paul, the former persecutor of the church who had inadvertently launched Philip into a lifetime of evangelism. Philip hosts him and the converts with him. Luke knew because he was one of the guests. Philip and Paul probably saw a lot of each other during the following two years when Paul was a prisoner in Caesarea (Acts 21:7-9).

Study 10. Crosscultural Evangelism. Acts 17:16-34.

Purpose: To learn how to give the gospel to someone with a different cultural background from our own.

Question 1. Paul must have toured some back streets! "Today, when we visit Athens and view the workmanship of the great architects and sculptors of the age of Pericles, we are free to admire them as works of art: to no one nowadays are they anything more. But in the first century of our era they were not viewed simply as works of art: they were temples and images of pagan deities" (F. F. Bruce, *Acts*, p. 349). The idols were an insult to God and meant eternal death for Athenians!

Question 2. In the synagogue were Jews and Greek God-fearers partially evangelized by their knowledge of God and the O.T. In the marketplace (*agora*), he would meet a cross-section of the population, including slaves and working people. Both dominant philosophies had degenerated. The Epicureans viewed sensual pleasure as the chief end in life, and the Stoics were pantheistic, rationalistic, self-sufficient and proud.

Question 3. A campus is a great place! Many large cities have dozens of foreign sections where you can visit shops, restaurants, temples and even foreign-language Christian congregations.

Question 4. The Greeks believed in the immortality of the soul but scoffed at the idea of the resurrection of the body (v. 32). The body was the soul's prison to be gotten rid of. Paul preached the "good news" about Jesus and his resurrection (v. 18). This is the core truth of the gospel, essential for all evangelism. Jesus is always the shortcut in evangelism (Jn 14:6). Without the resurrection even the crucifixion would have been in vain. For more information see the booklet *Evidence for the Resurrection* by J. N. D. Anderson (IVP).

Question 5. Paul compliments the Athenians for being religious. The Greeks superstitiously feared they might offend a god they overlooked. Hence the statue to the unknown deity.

Question 6. To begin with criticism would raise animosity and harden their resistance before they heard the gospel. All religions have some truth in them. For example, we might commend a Muslim for the importance they give to prayer. Or with someone who is involved in social work, we might notice how they care for the poor.

Question 7. Paul makes the following claims about the Athenians' overlooked deity—the Creator of heaven and earth and all that is in them. He is self-sufficient, needing no human help or human-made temples. He gives life to humans and has made all nationalities of one origin. He makes all the nations and decides their space on the planet and in history. But look at verse 27: why does he do all this? He's hoping people will search for him and find him! This glorious God is knowable and wants fellowship with his creatures. Dionysius and Damaris and others did "feel" after him and found him nearby—so near he could hear a whisper!

Question 8. Quoting their own sources could make them willing to consider the Scriptures. (Paul quotes other pagan poets in other letters.) The Athenian poet had said humans were a creator's offspring, reinforcing Paul's argument that the Creator must be significantly greater than the thing created and could in no way be stone or metal.

Question 9. Most good books and movies touch on ultimate issues. Os Guiness has given great lectures on Bergman's *Seventh Seal.* An English teacher used *Fiddler on the Roof* for evangelism. A pastor uses Russian literature.

Charles Colson says we should speak to people from within their own frame of reference. Instead of quoting the Bible on the big bang, just ask, "What was the cause behind it?" When someone says there is no absolute truth, ask how then they can be sure their belief about truth is true? People have to live in the world our God made, and only the Christian worldview makes sense of it. Others constantly butt their heads against reality.

Question 10. It would be too time-consuming here to consider what happens to people who haven't heard the gospel. God is fair to everyone. The Gentiles couldn't live up to the general revelation they received any more than the Jews could obey the law. Romans 3:23 says, "All have sinned and fall short of the glory of God." God had saved many people on credit, a debt which Jesus had now paid, so what mattered was how they responded to him (Rom 3:23-26). The question is not so much "Are they good or bad?" but "Are they dead or alive?" "How do they relate to Jesus?"

Question 11. Some Christians claim Paul failed in Athens because he was too intellectual. But this sermon is a sample of great, culturally sensitive preaching. More time was needed for sowing and watering before a harvest. But Paul probably established a church with converts from the Areopagus, the synagogue and the marketplace.

Study 11. Balanced Expectations. Mark 4:1-25.

Purpose: To gain insight into the results we can expect when we talk with people about Jesus.

Question 2. The story was no lesson on agriculture! Those with their minds made up could go home with their same prejudices. God gives us freedom to reject him if we insist. Parables were common, so all knew there was deeper meaning. Some would be disappointed, some spiritually hungry. Why didn't they ask? Most people hadn't really listened and didn't care.

Question 3. Jesus' healings during that long day should have made people hang on to every word. Some did come into the house with the disciples, asked (v. 10) and heard the interpretation.

Question 4. Parables must always be interpreted by their context. Matthew 13 puts this parable in a series which reinforce the same truths. People are evangelized when they have heard the gospel enough to know the consequences of receiving or rejecting Jesus Christ. He now does with this crowd what he taught in Matthew 7:6: "Neither give dogs what is sacred, nor cast your pearls to pigs." Hostile listeners mock precious truth and dissuade seekers. So Jesus gives crowds enough of his words and actions to fish out sincere seekers and teaches them "the secrets of the kingdom" in private. Also, he had to use some caution because of his many enemies.

Question 5. Understanding was essential. The Holy Spirit doesn't bypass our minds but acts on our whole inner person. We must not press for a decision on the basis of a gospel outline.

Question 9. Jesus was seeking the 25 percent--"the good soil"! Besides he had not given up on the hostile. Rebels could change. A few years later a first century Saul of Tarsus, the "the chief persecutor" of the church, became "the apostle to the Gentiles" and "our beloved brother Paul." He and Peter both emphasized fishing out seekers (Col 4:5-6; 1 Pet 3:14-17).

Question 10. Obedience to truth assures more truth. In Mark 4:12 Jesus quotes Isaiah 6:9-10 because the hostile leaders plotting to kill him were like those of Isaiah's day who became fixed in their unbelief—blind, deaf, incapable of spiritual response, doomed to exile in Babylon.

Question 11. Ways to prepare soil in individual evangelism include giving genuine friendship, answering intellectual objections, helping with distracting personal problems, allowing people to observe our conduct, letting them watch the interaction of a group of believers, removing fear by getting to know their family members. Use Bible study evangelism to give an adequate understanding of the gospel and loving follow-up (because full assurance often comes at that stage). Coach them into spiritual maturity.

Question 12. We have not failed because a conversation did not go well. We should "fish out" genuine seekers as Jesus did. But it is not a waste of time to speak to hardened people if we do not increase their hostility. At the Last

Judgment it will glorify Christ when every permanent rejecter has to admit he had ample opportunity to hear the truth. We should rejoice whenever we can turn people's thoughts to God, regardless of the response! J. I. Packer says *not* to "define evangelism in terms of an effect achieved in the lives of others; which amounts to saying that the essence of evangelizing is producing converts. . . . How then should evangelism be defined? The New Testament answer is very simple. According to the New Testament, evangelism is just preaching the gospel, the evangel" (*Evangelism and the Sovereignty of God* [Downers Grove: InterVarsity Press], 1961, pp. 40-41). Rejoice every time you can say a word for the Lord Jesus Christ!

Study 12. Facing Opposition. Acts 4:1-31.
Purpose: To learn to evangelize in persecution and draw on human and divine resources.
Questions 1-2. In the temple crowd 2,000 more men joined the church! The Sadducees, who controlled the temple and the priesthood, rejected resurrection. Peter blames the leaders for Jesus' crucifixion. But if Jesus was right, the clerics were wrong, and they stood to lose everything—social and political status, economic privilege, public reputation, religious influence. They could not afford to believe. They had to stamp out the "superstition."
Question 3. The gospel isn't insurance against adversity. The devil would charge God with fraud—with buying us off. (Remember Job?) Peter's letter says God values a tested faith. Our testimony is strongest in suffering. This is how God wins authorities—he loves them too. God can always protect us. So if he allows our arrest, we can *know* that he *will* use us with them (Rom 8:28).
Question 4. This was the Jewish supreme council who a few weeks earlier had Jesus crucified!
Question 6. The Holy Spirit is Christ in us. We receive the Spirit only once, but need frequent refills. Someone has said, "We leak!" For Luke the filling of the Spirit always results in speaking. There is no salvation except through Jesus. People are offended by the exclusiveness of biblical Christianity but our faith is *exclusive, unique* and *superior* to all religions. Jesus is no religious leader but the Creator of the universe and Lord over all who believe in him and over all who do not believe! All will answer to him.
Question 7. Peter and John were rustic fishermen, but they were not illiterate. The clerics were surprised at Peter's powerful preaching and his knowledge of Scripture, when he had no formal rabbinical training. But they could tell both men had been with Jesus. Jesus was there, in them! They also reflected his training and spiritual authority.
Question 8. The authorities at the trial were stuck. Peter's exhibit A was standing beside him. All of Jerusalem marveled at this healing. The Jesus movement had become immensely popular. People were resentful of their

religious leaders' role in the crucifixion. Peter respectfully asks *them* to decide if he and John should disobey God! No circumstance ever excuses us from witnessing to Jesus Christ, although we must not flaunt it in the face of civil authorities, as we will see in 1 Peter.

Question 9. We don't know if one person prayed and all said "amens," or if this was a composite prayer with spontaneous, Spirit-guided contributions from several people (conversational prayer!). But God is sovereign, Creator and Sustainer of all. Jesus was God's anointed one, his promised King. They used Scripture. Christians need group prayer as well as individual prayer.

Question 10. The Christians prayed for boldness because they were highly motivated to make Jesus Christ known. They rejoiced in his kingship and his kingdom. Evangelism should not be deliberately confrontational—a low-key approach is more effective. We should always be gracious, gentle (Col 4:4-5; 2 Tim 2:24-26). We may persuade with reasons but not debate with animosity. John Stott says, "This injunction is not to be taken as an excuse for the insensitive brashness which has sometimes characterized our evangelism and brought it into disrepute"(*The Message of 2 Timothy* [InterVarsity Press, 1973], p. 107). Tony Campolo says, "Don't let your evangelism embarrass God!"

Question 11. Many believers and foreign, self-supporting "tentmaker" missionaries make Jesus Christ known in spiritually hostile countries. To inadvertently approach the wrong person can result in arrest, prison, job loss, expulsion from the country and even death. They must evangelize but not flaunt their religion. They must "fish out" the spiritually thirsty seekers and answer their questions privately. What joy to tell the gospel to those who long to hear it! Their questions give us insights into them and show us how to proceed to disciple them to Jesus Christ. This selective, nonintrusive evangelism was also taught by Paul (Col 4:5, 6) and used by Jesus (Mk 4).

Question 12. We reverence Jesus Christ in our hearts, take part in worship, are conscious of his presence, count on his help and allow him to speak and act through us. Seekers sense his presence!

Question 13. What secret enabled the Christians to be courageous, joyful and gracious even as they suffered physical and economic loss? It was the Spirit of Jesus in them! Paul says the mystery of the ages now revealed is— "Christ in you, the hope of glory" (Col 1:27; 1 Jn 5:11-12; Rom 8:8-9).

Rebecca Manley Pippert is the author of Out of the Saltshaker *and a popular speaker living in the Chicago suburbs. Ruth Siemens spent twenty-one years pioneering IFES campus fellowships in Latin America and Europe, and founded Global Opportunities, which helps missions-motivated Christians support themselves abroad as they integrate work and witness.*